Divine Inspirations

Divine Inspirations

Pearls of Bible Wisdom from the
Old and New Testaments

COMPILED BY ANNE PIERCE

Edited by Reverend Dr. John Mark Goerss,
Reverend James R. Pierce, and
Reverend Chestina Mitchell Archibald

With wood engravings from designs of
Fra Angelico, Pietro Perugino,
Francesco Francia, Fra Bartolommeo, Titian,
Raphael, Daniel di Volterra, and others

Produced by The Philip Lief Group, Inc.
CASTLE BOOKS

This edition published by arrangement with HarperCollins*Publishers*, Inc. All rights reserved.

Produced by the Philip Lief Group. Inc.

Published by
Castle Books,
a division of Book Sales, Inc.
114 Northfield Avenue
Edison, New Jersey 08837

Printed in the United States of America

ISBN 0-7858-1149-4

Contents

Introduction

===

As the Good Book reminds us, "If any of you needs wisdom, you should ask God, and it shall be given to you. God is generous and won't correct you for the asking." (James 1:5).

The gift of wisdom can open you up to a world of possibilities and hope. You now hold in your hands a new source culled from the fountain from which all wisdom flows: the Holy Bible. We have carefully scrutinized the Old and New Testaments, searching for quotable, inspiring passages that hold deep, relevant meaning for us and the world we live in today. The result: a tremendously versatile wealth of insight, uniquely organized to help you meet the many joys and challenges you face in your life.

The book is arranged alphabetically by subject, spanning categories from "Acceptance" and "Compassion," to "Self-esteem," "Tolerance," and "Wealth." The categories themselves reflect the concerns, circumstances, and emotions most common to the contemporary reader and best suited to distilling as much of the Bible's teachings as possible. To spark more refined searching, and to underscore the manner in which the Bible interweaves related concepts, we have provided cross-references to other headings where related quotations might be found.

Once you have opened to a specific category, you will discover that the quotations have been arranged under the subject headings in the order in which they appear in the Bible. Every quotation also contains a citation—chapter and verse. The abbreviations following the quotations indicate the translation used. The following is a key to the abbreviations:

(CEV)	Contemporary English Version
(GNB)	Good News Bible
(KJV)	King James Version
(NASB)	New American Standard Bible
(NIV)	New International Version
(NJB)	New Jerusalem Bible
(NRSV)	New Revised Standard Version
(TEV)	Today's English Version
(TLB)	The Living Bible

The artwork bordering the nuggets of truth contained within these pages are exquisite engravings on wood from designs of immortal Italian artists, including Fra Angelico, Pietro Perugino, Francesco Francia, Lorenzo di Credi, Raphael, and many others.

We invite you to turn to these pages for divine enlightenment in any situation—whether you are seeking a way to impart life lessons to a child (see ROLE MODELS: "Don't let anyone make fun of you, just because you are young. Set an example to other followers by what you say and do, as well as by your love, faith, and purity." 1 Timothy 4:12); working through a difficult situation at the office (see PERSEVERANCE: "Blessed is the man who perseveres under trial, because when he has stood the test, he will receive the crown of life that God has promised to those who love him." James 1:12); or simply to find an uplifting, new way to look at your world (*see* GOODNESS: "Refuse no kindness to those who have a right to it, if it is in your power to perform it." Proverbs 3:27).

While perusing this book, you will most likely become reacquainted with some familiar quotations, and you are almost certain to encounter many others for the first time. Within each category, you will also observe a wide range of shades and meanings pertaining to the subject at hand. This fascinating juxtaposition of contradictory quotations (and, in some instances, the resonating effect of similar ones) can serve as the first step of a stimulating path. While the primary aim of this book is to put at-a-glance biblical wisdom at your fingertips, we hope our compilation may encourage you and your loved ones to pursue a more detailed exploration of the questions and issues these shimmering quotations may raise.

Acceptance
(*see also* PATIENCE *and* TOLERANCE)

Let the words of my mouth and meditation of my heart be acceptable in thy sight, O Lord, my strength and my redeemer. Psalms 19:14 (KJV)

I tell for certain that anyone who welcomes my messengers also welcomes me, and anyone who welcomes me welcomes the one who sent me. John 13:20 (CEV)

Then Peter began to speak: "I now realize how true it is that God does not show favoritism, but accepts men from every nation who fear him and do what is right." Acts 10:34–35 (NIV)

Welcome all the Lord's followers, even those whose faith is weak. Don't criticize them for having beliefs that are different from yours. Romans 14:1 (CEV)

Let not him who eats regard with contempt him who does not eat, and let not him who does not eat judge him who eats, for God has accepted him. Romans 14:3 (NASB)

Accept one another, then, for the sake of God's glory, as Christ accepted you. Romans 15:7 (NJB)

I am not complaining about having too little. I have learned to be satisfied with whatever I have. Philippians 4:11 (CEV)

Action

(*see also* PRODUCTIVITY, SELF-SUFFICIENCY, *and* WORK ETHIC)

A young man's character is in what he does, if his behavior is pure and straight.
Proverbs 20:11 (NJB)

Your light must shine before people so that they will see the good things you do and praise your Father in heaven.
Matthew 5:16 (GNB)

Each one should test his own actions. Then he can take pride in himself, without comparing himself to somebody else, for each one should carry his own load. Galatians 6:4–5 (NIV)

But be ye doers of the word, and not hearers only, deceiving your own selves.
James 1:22 (KJV)

But one who looks intently at the perfect law, the law of liberty, and abides by it, not having become a forgetful hearer but an effectual doer, this man shall be blessed in what he does.
James 1:25 (NASB)

Faith, if good deeds do not go with it, is quite dead.
James 2:17 (NJB)

I pray that your fellowship in faith may come to expression in full knowledge of all the good we can do in Christ. Philemon 6 (NJB)

Children, you show your love for others by truly

helping them, and not by merely talking about it.
1 John 3:18 (CEV)

Adversity

(*see also* TROUBLED TIMES)

Many are the afflictions of the righteous; but the Lord delivers him out of them all. Psalms 34:19 (NASB)

God is our refuge and strength, a very present help in trouble. Psalms 46:1 (KJV)

The Lord preserves the simple; I was brought low, and He saved me. Psalms 116:6 (NASB)

Don't give up and be helpless in times of trouble.
Proverbs 24:10 (CEV)

Better is a dish of vegetables where love is, than a fattened ox and hatred with it.
Proverbs 15:17 (NASB)

A friend loveth at all times, and a brother is born for adversity. Proverbs 17:17 (KJV)

Drive out the scoffer, and contention will go out, even strife and dishonor will cease. Proverbs 22:10 (NASB)

We are hard pressed on every side, but not crushed; perplexed, but not in despair; persecuted, but not abandoned; struck down, but not destroyed.

2 Corinthians 4:8–9 (NIV)

Rejoice in hope, be patient in suffering, persevere in prayer. Romans 12:12 (NRSV)

Even though now for a little while, you have been distressed by various trials . . . the proof of your faith, being more precious than gold which is perishable . . . may be found to result in praise and glory and honor at the revelation of Jesus Christ. 1 Peter 1:6–7 (NASB)

Do not be afraid of the sufferings that are coming to you. Look, the devil will send some of you to prison to put you to the test, and you must face hardship for ten days. Even if you have to die, remain faithful, and I will give you the crown of life for a prize. Revelation 2:10 (NJB)

Aging
(*see also* DEATH *and* LIFE)

Thou shalt be buried in a good old age. Genesis 15:15 (KJV)

You shall rise up before the grayheaded, and

honor the aged, and you shall revere your God; I am the Lord. Leviticus 19:32 (NASB)

Although Moses was one hundred and twenty years old when he died, his eye was not dim, nor his vigor abated. Deuteronomy 34:7 (NASB)

I thought age should speak, and increased years should teach wisdom. Job 32:7 (NASB)

As long as I can remember, good people have never been left helpless, and their children have never gone

begging for food. Psalms 37:25 (CEV)

Beloved, thou hast made my days as handbreadths; and mine age is as nothing before thee. Psalms 39:5 (KJV)

We spend our years as a tale that is told. Psalms 90:9 (KJV)

So teach us to number our days, that we may apply our hearts unto wisdom. Psalms 92:14 (KJV)

They shall still bring forth fruit in old age. Psalms 90:12 (KJV)

The crown of the aged is their children's children. Proverbs 17:6 (NJB)

Remember also your Creator in the days of your youth, before the evil days come and the years draw near when you will say, "I have no delight in them." Ecclesiastes 12:1 (NASB)

And even to your old age I am He; and even to gray hairs will I carry you. Isaiah 46:4 (KJV)

Your old men shall dream dreams. Joel 2:28 (NRSV)

Do not rebuke an older man harshly, but exhort him as if he were your father. Treat younger men as brothers, older women as mothers, and younger women as sisters, with absolute purity. 1 Timothy 5:1–2 (NIV)

Ambition

And seekest thou great things for thyself? Seek them not. Jeremiah 45:5 (KJV)

The last shall be first, and the first last. Matthew 20:16 (KJV)

Do nothing out of selfish ambition or vain conceit, but in humility consider others better than yourselves. Philippians 2:3 (NIV)

Try your best to live quietly, and to mind your own business, and to work hard, just as we are taught to do. 1 Thessalonians 4:11 (CEV)

It is true that anyone who desires to be a church official wants to be something worthwhile. 1 Timothy 3:1 (CEV)

Angels

The Lord . . . will send his angels before you. Genesis 24:7 (NRSV)

Seraphim stood above Him, each having six wings; with two he covered his face, and with two he covered his feet, and with two he flew. And one called out to another and said, "Holy, Holy, Holy, is the Lord of hosts, the whole earth is full of His glory." Isaiah 6:2–3 (NASB)

If you honor the Lord, his angel will protect you. Psalms 34:7 (CEV)

The angel said to her, "Do not be afraid, Mary, for you have found favor with God." Luke 1:30 (NRSV)

But the angel said to them, "Do not be afraid, for see—I am bringing you good news of great joy for all people." Luke 2:10 (NRSV)

For it is written: "He will command his angels concerning you to guard you carefully; they will lift you up in their hands, so that you will not strike your foot against a stone." Luke 4:10–11 (NIV)

Be sure to welcome strangers into your home. By doing this, some people have welcomed angels as guests, without even knowing it. Hebrews 13:2 (CEV)

The seven angels that had seven trumpets now made ready to sound them. Revelation 8:6 (NJB)

Anger
(*see also* ACCEPTANCE)

The Lord is compassionate and gracious, slow to anger and abounding in love. Psalms 103:8 (NASB)

Those with good sense are slow to anger, and it is their glory to overlook an offense. Proverbs 19:11 (NRSV)

Sneering at other people is a spark that sets a city on fire; using good sense can put out the flames of anger. Proverbs 29:8 (CEV)

Only fools get quickly angry and hold a grudge. Ecclesiastes 7:9 (CEV)

In your anger do not sin: Do not let the sun go down while you are still angry, and do not give the devil a foothold. Ephesians 4:26–27 (NIV)

Anxiety
(*see also* FEAR, PATIENCE, STRESS, TESTS, *and* TROUBLED TIMES)

Cast your burden upon the Lord, and He will sustain you; He will never allow the righteous to be shaken. Psalms 55:22 (NASB)

When my anxious thoughts multiply within me, thy consolations delight my soul. Psalms 94:19 (NASB)

Worry makes a heart heavy,
a kindly word makes it glad.
Proverbs 12:25 (NJB)

For this reason I say to you,
do not be anxious for your
life, as to what you shall eat,
or what you shall drink; nor
for your body, as to what
you shall put on. Is not life
more than food, and the
body than clothing?
Matthew 6:25 (NASB)

Don't worry about
tomorrow. It will take care
of itself. You have enough to
worry about today.
Matthew 6:34 (CEV)

Don't worry about anything,
but pray about everything.
With thankful hearts offer up
your prayers and requests to
God. Philippians 4:6 (CEV)

Cast all your anxiety upon
Him, because He cares for
you. 1 Peter 5:7 (NASB)

Appearances
(*see also* BEAUTY, CHAR-
ACTER, *and* SELF-IMAGE)

But the Lord said to Samuel,
"Do not consider his appearance or his height, for I have
rejected him. The Lord does
not look at the things man
looks at. Man looks at the
outward appearance, but the
Lord looks at the heart."
1 Samuel 16:7 (NIV)

Do not judge by appearances,
but judge with right judgment. John 7:24 (NRSV)

The Scriptures say, "If you want to brag, then brag about the Lord." 2 Corinthians 10:17 (CEV)

Attitude

When things are going well, enjoy yourself, and when they are going badly, consider this: God has designed the one no less than the other so that we should take nothing for granted. Ecclesiastes 7:14 (NJB)

Good people bring good things out of their hearts, but evil people bring evil things out of their hearts. Matthew 12:35 (CEV)

I have told you all this so that you may find peace in me. In the world you will have hardship, but be courageous: I have conquered the world. John 16:33 (NJB)

Each of you must make up your own mind about how much to give. But don't feel sorry that you must give and don't feel that you are forced to give. God loves people who love to give. 2 Corinthians 9:7 (CEV)

As God's chosen ones, holy and beloved, clothe yourselves with compassion, kindness, humility, meekness and patience. Colossians 3:12 (NRSV)

Your attitude should be the same as that of Christ Jesus:

Who, being in very nature God, did not consider equality with God something to be grasped, but made himself nothing, taking the very nature of a servant, being made in human likeness. Philippians 2:5–7 (NIV)

To those who are pure themselves, everything is pure; but to those who have been corrupted and lack faith nothing can be pure—the corruption is both in their minds and their consciences. Titus 1:15 (NJB)

Be clothed with humility. 1 Peter 5:5 (KJV)

Beauty

(*see also* APPEARANCES *and* SELF-IMAGE)

Out of Zion, the perfection of beauty, God shines forth. Psalms 50:2 (NRSV)

One thing I have asked from the Lord, that I shall seek: That I may dwell in the house of the Lord all the days of my life, to behold the beauty of the Lord, and to meditate in His temple. Psalms 27:4 (NASB)

Charm is deceitful, and beauty is vain, but a woman who fears the Lord is to be praised. Proverbs 31:30 (NRSV)

He hath made everything beautiful in his time. Ecclesiastes 3:11 (KJV)

And why are you anxious about clothing? Observe how the lilies of the field grow; they do not toil nor do they spin, yet I say to you that even Solomon in all his glory did not clothe himself like one of these. Matthew 6:28–9 (NASB)

It is a beautiful sight to see even the feet of someone coming to preach the good news. Romans 10:15 (CEV)

Your beauty should not come from outward adornment, such as braided hair and the wearing of gold jewelry and fine clothes. Instead, it should be that of your inner self, the unfading beauty of a gentle and quiet spirit, which is of great worth in God's sight. 1 Peter 3:3–4 (NIV)

Belief
(*see also* FAITHFULNESS)

And He said to them, "Why are you timid, you men of little faith?" Then He arose, and rebuked the winds and the sea; and it became

12

perfectly calm.
Matthew 8:26 (NASB)

But Jesus turning and seeing her said, "Daughter, take courage; your faith has made you well." And at once the woman was made well. Matthew 9:22 (NASB)

And He said to them, "Because of the littleness of your faith; for truly I say to you, if you have faith as a mustard seed, you shall say to this mountain, 'Move from here to there,' and it shall move; and nothing shall be impossible to you." Matthew 17:20 (NASB)

If you have faith when you pray, you will be given whatever you ask for. Matthew 21:22 (CEV)

Repent, and believe in the good news. Mark 1:15 (NRSV)

Do not fear, only believe. Mark 5:26 (NRSV)

Jesus replied, ". . . Anything is possible for someone who has faith!" Mark 9:23 (CEV)

Lord, I believe; help thou mine unbelief. Mark 9:24 (KJV)

Yes, blessed is she who believed that the

promise made her by the Lord would be fulfilled. Luke 1:45 (NJB)

Yet to all who received him, to those who believed in his name, he gave the right to become children of God. John 1:12 (NIV)

For God so loved the world, that He gave His only begotten Son, that whoever believes in Him should not perish, but have eternal life. John 3:16 (NASB)

Truly, truly, I say to you, he who hears My word, and believes Him who sent Me, has eternal life, and does not come into judgment, but has passed out of death into life. John 5:24 (NASB)

How could you possibly believe? You have to have your friends praise you, and you don't care about the praise that only God can give! John 5:44 (CEV)

Jesus said to them, "I am the bread of life; he who comes to Me shall not hunger, and he who believes in Me shall never thirst." John 6:35 (NASB)

Jesus said to her, I am the resurrection and the life, those who believe in me, even though they die will live, and everyone who lives and believes in me will never die. John 11:25–26 (NRSV)

Do not let your hearts be troubled. Believe in God,

14

believe also in me. John 14:1 (NRSV)

Then saith he to Thomas, "Reach hither thy finger, and behold my hands; and reach hither thy hand and thrust it into my side: and be not faithless, but believing. And Thomas answered and said unto him, "My Lord and my God." Jesus saith unto him, "Thomas, because thou hast seen me, thou hast believed: blessed are they that have not seen, and yet have believed." John 20:27–9 (KJV)

But it is in that way faith comes, from hearing, and that means hearing the word of Christ. Romans 10:17 (NJB)

We live by faith, not by sight. 2 Corinthians 5:7 (CEV)

Faith makes us sure of what we hope for and gives us proof of what we cannot see. Hebrews 11:1 (CEV)

And without faith it is impossible to please Him, for he who comes to God must believe that He is, and that He is a rewarder of those who seek Him. Hebrews 11:6 (NASB)

Blame

(see also FAULTS, FORGIVENESS, JUDGMENT, and RESPONSIBILITY)

The man said, "The woman you put here with me she gave me some fruit from the tree, and I ate it." Then the Lord God said to the woman, "What is this you have done?" The woman said, "The serpent deceived me, and I ate." Genesis 3:12–13 (NIV)

You must be blameless before God. Deuteronomy 18:13 (CEV)

When they kept on questioning him, he straightened up and said to them, "If any one of you is without sin, let him be the first to throw a stone at her." John 8:7 (NIV)

As he went along, he saw a man blind from birth. His disciples asked him, "Rabbi, who sinned, this man or his parents, that he was born blind?" "Neither this man nor his parents sinned," said Jesus, "but this happened so that the work of God might be displayed in his life." John 9:1–3 (NIV)

He will also strengthen you to the end, so that you will be blameless on the day of our Lord Jesus Christ. 1 Corinthians 1:8 (NRSV)

Blessings
(see also GRATITUDE, PRAISING GOD, *and* REWARDS)

And I will make you a great nation, and I will bless you,

and make your name great;
and so you shall be a
blessing; and I will bless
those who bless you, and the
one who curses you I will
curse. And in you all the
families of the earth shall be
blessed. Genesis 12:2–3
(NASB)

Blessings of the grains and
flowers, blessings of the
eternal mountains, bounty of
the everlasting hills—may
they descend . . . on the
crown of the one dedicated
from among his brothers!
Genesis 49:26 (NJB)

Dedicate yourselves today to
the Lord . . . in order that
He may bestow a blessing
upon you today." Exodus
32:29 (NASB)

There also you and your
households shall eat before
the Lord your God, and
rejoice in all your undertakings in which the Lord your
God has blessed you.
Deuteronomy 12:7 (NASB)

Every man shall give as he is
able, according to the
blessing of the Lord your
God which He has given
you. Deuteronomy 30:19
(NASB)

I have set before you life and
death, blessings and curses.
Choose life so that you and
your descendants may live.
Deuteronomy 16:17 (NRSV)

You confer on him everlasting
blessings, you gladden him
with the joy of your presence. Psalms 21:6 (NJB)

Bless the Lord, O my soul, and all that is within me; bless his holy name. Bless the Lord, O my soul, do not forget all his benefits. Psalms 103:1-2 (NRSV)

"Bring the whole tithe into the storehouse, that there may be food in my house. Test me in this," says the Lord Almighty, "and see if I will not throw open the floodgates of heaven and pour out so much blessing that you will not have room enough for it." Malachi 3:10 (NIV)

Because of all that the Son is, we have been given one blessing after another. John 1:16 (CEV)

Praise the God and Father of our Lord Jesus Christ for the spiritual blessings that Christ has brought us from heaven! Ephesians 1:3 (CEV)

Calm
(see also PEACE)

Fret not thyself of evildoers neither by the enviousness of the workers of iniquity. Be still, and know that I am God. Psalms 37:1 (KJV)

The hot-headed provokes disputes, the equable allays dissension. Proverbs 15:18 (NJB)

Be still, and know that I am God. Proverbs 46:10 (KJV)

Let us therefore follow after the things which make for peace. Romans 14:19 (KJV)

You ought to keep calm and to do nothing rash. Acts 19:36 (NASB)

The fruit of the Spirit is love, joy, and peace. Galatians 5:22 (KJV)

If the anger of a ruler rises against you, do not leave your post; composure mitigates grave offenses. Ecclesiastes 10:4 (NJB)

Character
(*see also* APPEARANCES, ATTITUDE, HONESTY, *and* PEOPLE OF GOD)

Better is the poor who walks in his integrity, than he who is crooked though he be rich. Proverbs 28:6 (NASB)

For he will be like a tree planted by the water, that extends its roots by a stream and will not fear when the heat comes; but its leaves will be green, and it will not be anxious in a year of drought nor cease to yield fruit. Jeremiah 17:8 (NASB)

But I say to you, do not resist him who is evil; but whoever slaps you on your right cheek, turn to him the other also. Matthew 5:39 (NASB)

But I tell you to love your enemies and pray for anyone who mistreats you. Matthew 5:44 (CEV)

And not only this, but we also exult in our tribulations, knowing that tribulation brings about perseverance; and perseverance, proven character; and proven character, hope. Romans 5:3–4 (NASB)

If our strength is strong, we should be patient with the Lord's followers whose faith is weak. Romans 15:1 (CEV)

But by the grace of God I am what I am, and His grace toward me did not prove vain; but I labored even more than all of them, yet not I, but the grace of God with me. 1 Corinthians 15:10 (NASB)

My grace is sufficient for you, for power is made perfect in weakness. 2 Corinthians 12:9 (NRSV)

Do all things without grumbling or disputing. Philippians 2:14 (NASB)

If we say we have no sin, we deceive ourselves, and the truth is not in us. 1 John 1:8 (KJV)

Children
(*see also* FAMILY *and* PARENTING)

With praises from children and from tiny infants, you have built a fortress. It makes your enemies silent, and all who turn against you are left speechless. Psalms 8:2 (CEV)

Teach children how they should live, and they will remember it all their life. Proverbs 22:6 (GNB)

And when you welcome . . . children because of me, you welcome me. Matthew 18:5 (CEV)

Then little children were being brought to him in order that he might lay hands on them and pray. The disciples spoke sternly to those who brought them; but Jesus said, "Let the little children come to me, and do not stop them for it is to such as these the kingdom of heaven belongs." Matthew 19:13-14 (NRSV)

I tell you the truth, anyone who will not receive the kingdom of God like a little child will never enter it. Mark 10:15 (NIV)

When I was a child, my speech, feelings, and thinking were that of a child; now that I am an adult, I have no more use for childish

ways. 1 Corinthians 13:11 (GNB)

Children, obey your parents in the Lord, for this is right. "Honor your father and mother"—which is the first commandment with a promise—"that it may go well with you and that you may enjoy long life on the earth." Ephesians 6:1–3 (NIV)

Children, obey your parents in everything, for this is your acceptable duty in the Lord. Colossians 3:20 (NRSV)

I have no greater joy than this, to hear of my children walking in the truth. 3 John 4 (NASB)

Comfort

(*see also* CALM, FEAR, GRIEF, PRAYER, SECURITY, *and* TROUBLED TIMES)

Yea, thou I walk through the valley of the shadow of death, I will fear no evil: for thou art with me; thy rod and thy staff they comfort me. Psalms 23:4 (KJV)

I have kept your age-old judgments in mind, Lord, and I am comforted. Psalms 119:52 (NJB)

I serve you, Lord. Comfort me with your love, just as you have promised. Psalms 119:76 (CEV)

"Comfort, O comfort My people," says your God. "Speak kindly to Jerusalem;

22

and call out to her, that her warfare has ended, that her iniquity has been removed, that she has received of the Lord's hand double for all her sins." Isaiah 40:1–2 (NRSV)

As one whom his mother comforts, so I will comfort you; And you shall be comforted in Jerusalem. Isaiah 66:13 (NASB)

Blessed are those who mourn, for they shall be comforted. Matthew 5:4 (NASB)

Praise be to the God and Father of our Lord Jesus Christ, the Father of compassion and the God of all comfort, who comforts us in all our troubles, so that we can comfort those in any

trouble with the comfort we ourselves have received from God. 2 Corinthians 1:3–4 (NIV)

Commitment
(*see also* DUTY, PERSEVER-ANCE, *and* RESPONSIBILITY)

I will die where you die and be buried beside you. May the Lord punish me if we are ever separated, even by death! Ruth 1:17 (CEV)

And Jonathan made David vow again because of his love for him, because he loved him as he loved his own life. 1 Samuel 20:17 (NASB)

As the Lord lives and as you yourself live, I will not leave you. 2 Kings 2:2 (NASB)

He who pursues righteousness and loyalty finds life, righteousness and honor. Proverbs 21:21 (NASB)

I am his, and he is mine, as he feeds his sheep among the lilies. Song 6:3 (CEV)

I will betroth you to me forever; I will betroth you in righteousness and justice, in love and compassion. Hosea 2:19 (NIV)

Peter spoke up, "Even if all the others reject you, I never will." Matthew 26:33 (NIV)

Companionship

(*see also* FRIENDSHIP *and* RELATIONSHIPS)

David and Saul finished talking, and soon David and Jonathan became best friends. Jonathan thought as much of David as he did of himself. 1 Samuel 18:1 (CEV)

Blessed is the man who does not walk in the counsel of the wicked or stand in the way of sinners or sit in the seat of mockers. Psalms 1:1 (NIV)

A man of many friends comes to ruin, but there is a friend who sticks closer than a brother. Proverbs 18:24 (NASB)

Compassion

(*see also* COMFORT, GENEROSITY, LISTENING, MERCY, *and* SUFFERING)

May God Almighty grant you compassion in the sight of the man, that he may release to you your other brother and Benjamin. And as for me, if I am bereaved of my children, I am bereaved. Genesis 43:14 (NASB)

The Lord is compassionate and gracious, slow to anger, abounding in love. Psalms 103:8 (NIV)

Shout for joy, O heavens; rejoice, O earth; burst into song, O mountains! For the Lord comforts his people and will have compassion on his afflicted ones. Zechariah 7:9 (NIV)

Thus has the Lord of hosts said, "Dispense true justice, and practice kindness and compassion each to his brother." Isaiah 49:13 (NASB)

As the chosen of God, then, the holy people whom he loves, you are clothed in heartfelt compassion, in generosity and humility, gentleness and patience. Colossians 3:12 (NJB)

Finally, all of you should agree and have concern and love for each other. You should also be kind and humble. 1 Peter 3:8 (CEV)

25

Competition

Another thing I have observed under the sun: that the race is not won by the speediest, nor the battle by the champions; it is not the wise who get food, nor the intelligent wealth, nor the learned favor: chance and mischance befall them all. Ecclesiastes 9:11 (NJB)

If you have run with footmen and they have tired you out, then how can you compete with horses? Jeremiah 12:5 (NASB)

But many who are now first will be last, and many who are last will be first. Matthew 19:30 (CEV)

Everyone who competes in the games goes into strict training. They do it to get a crown that will not last; but we do it to get a crown that will last forever. 1 Corinthians 9:25 (NIV)

And also if anyone competes as an athlete, he does not win the prize unless he competes according to the rules. 2 Timothy 2:5 (NASB)

We . . . should throw off everything that weighs us down and the sin that clings so closely, and with perseverance keep running in the race that lies ahead of us. Hebrews 12:1 (NJB)

Courage
(*see also* FEAR *and* STRENGTH)

Be strong, stand firm, do not be afraid of them, for the Lord your God is going with you; he will not fail or desert you. Deuteronomy 31:6 (NJB)

Joshua then said to them, "Do not fear or be dismayed! Be strong and courageous, for thus the Lord will do to all your enemies with whom you fight." Joshua 10:25 (NASB)

Be strong, and let us show ourselves courageous for the sake of our people and for the cities of our God; and may the Lord do what is good in His sight. 2 Samuel 10:12 (NASB)

Then you shall prosper, if you are careful to observe the statutes and the ordinances which the Lord commanded Moses concerning Israel. Be strong and courageous, do not fear nor be dismayed. 1 Chronicles 22:13 (NASB)

Say to the faint-hearted, Be strong! Do not be afraid. Here is your God, vengeance is coming, divine retribution; he is coming to save you. Isaiah 35:4 (NJB)

But as for me, I will watch expectantly for the Lord; I will wait for the God of my salvation. My God will hear me. Micah 7:7 (NASB)

Jesus turned. He saw the woman and said, "Don't worry! You are now well

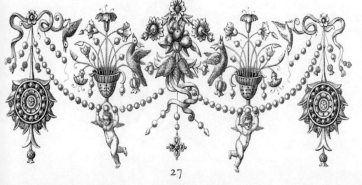

because of your faith." At that moment she was healed. Matthew 9:22 (CEV)

When they saw the courage of Peter and John and realized that they were unschooled, ordinary men, they were astonished and they took note that these men had been with Jesus. Acts 4:13 (NIV)

Therefore, being always of good courage, and knowing that while we are at home in the body we are absent from the Lord—for we walk by faith, not by sight—we are of good courage, I say, and prefer rather to be absent from the body and to be at home with the Lord. 2 Corinthians 5:6–8 (NASB)

I honestly expect and hope that I will never do anything to be ashamed of. Whether I live or die, I always want to be as brave as I am now and bring honor to Christ. Philippians 1:20 (CEV)

I can do all things through him who strengthens me. Philippians 4:13 (NRSV)

Creativity

O Lord, how manifold are your works! In wisdom you have made them all; the earth is full of your creatures. Psalms 104:24 (NRSV)

I see there is no contentment for a human being except happiness in achievement; such is the lot of all human beings. No one can tell us what will happen after we are gone. Ecclesiastes 3:22 (NJB)

See, I am doing a new thing! Now it springs up; do you not perceive it? I am making a way in the desert and streams in the wasteland. Isaiah 43:19 (NIV)

My Father has given me everything, and he is the only one who knows the Son. But the Son wants to tell others about the Father, so that they can know him too. Luke 10:22 (CEV)

Of course, every house is built by someone, and God is really the one who built everything. Hebrews 3:4 (CEV)

Then the One sitting on the throne spoke. "Look, I am making the whole of creation new." Write this, "What I am saying is trustworthy and will come true." Revelation 21:5 (NJB)

Death
(*see also* AGING *and* LIFE)

For dust thou art, and unto dust shalt thou return. Genesis 3:19 (NASB)

Let me die the death of the upright, and let my end be like his! Numbers 23:10 (NASB)

The waves of death swirled about me; the torrents of destruction overwhelmed me. The cords of the grave coiled around me; the snares of death confronted me. He reached down from on high and took hold of me; he drew me out of deep waters. 2 Samuel 22:5–6, 17 (NASB)

The God gave, and the Lord hath taken away; blessed be the name of the Lord. Job 1:21 (KJV)

Yea, thou I walk through the valley of the shadow of death, I will fear no evil: for thou art with me; thy rod and thy staff they comfort me. Psalms 23:4 (KJV)

For Thou hast delivered my soul from death, indeed my feet from stumbling, so that I may walk before God in the light of the living. Psalms 56:13 (NASB)

What you gain by doing evil won't help you at all, but being good can save you from death. Proverbs 10:2 (CEV)

The wise have their eyes open, the fool walks in the dark. And yet I know that one fate befalls them both. Ecclesiastes 2:14 (NJB)

A time to be born and a time to die. Ecclesiastes 3:2 (KJV)

It is better to go to a house of mourning than to go to a house of feasting, for death is the destiny of every man; the living should take this to heart. Ecclesiastes 7:2 (NIV)

Put me like a seal over your heart, like a seal on your arm. For love is as strong as death. Song of Songs 8:6 (NASB)

He will swallow up death for all time, and the Lord God will wipe tears away from all faces, and He will remove the reproach of His people from all the earth; for the Lord has spoken. Isaiah 25:8 (NASB)

That whosoever believeth in Him should not perish, but have everlasting life. John 3:16 (KJV)

Blessed are the dead which die in the Lord. Revelation 14:13 (KJV)

And God shall wipe away all tears from their eyes; and there shall be no more death, neither sorrow, nor crying, neither shall there be any more pain: for the former things have passed away. Revelation 21:4 (KJV)

Decisions
(see also COURAGE and GUIDANCE)

Choose for yourselves this day whom you will serve. Joshua 24:15 (NIV)

Choose life in order that you may live . . . for this is your life and the length of your days, that you may live in the land of the Lord.

Deuteronomy
30:19–20 (NASB)

Let us choose for ourselves what is right; let us know among ourselves what is good.
Job 34:4 (NASB)

We make our own decisions, but the Lord alone determines what happens. Proverbs 16:33 (CEV)

The poor and needy will be treated with fairness and justice. Isaiah 11:4 (CEV)

If I did judge, I would judge fairly, because I would not be doing it alone. The Father who sent me here is with me. John 8:16 (CEV)

So then, brothers and sisters, we are debtor, not to the flesh, to live according to the flesh. Romans 8:12 (NRSV)

Owe no one anything, except to love one another. Romans 13:8 (NRSV)

If I am to go on living in the body, this will mean fruitful labor for me. Yet what shall I choose? I do not know! I am torn between the two: I desire to depart and be with Christ, which is better by far; but it is more necessary for you that I remain in the body. Philippians 1:22–24 (NIV)

Anyone who doubts is like an ocean wave tossed around in a storm. If you are that kind of person, you can't make up your mind, and you surely can't be trusted. So don't expect the Lord to give you anything at all. James 1:7–8 (CEV)

Desire

(*see also* HEART *and* LOVE)

You shall not covet your neighbor's wife, and you shall not desire your neighbor's house, his field or his male ser-vant or his female servant, his ox or his donkey or anything that belongs to your neighbor. Deuteronomy 5:21 (NASB)

O Lord, Thou hast heard the desire of the humble; Thou wilt strengthen their heart. Psalms 10:17 (NASB)

Do what the Lord wants, and he will give your heart's desire. Psalms 37:4 (CEV)

Thou desirest not sacrifice; else I would give it. Psalms 51:16 (KJV)

You open your hand, satisfying the desire of every living thing. Psalms 145:16 (NRSV)

He fulfills the desires of those who fear him, he hears their cry and saves them. Psalms 145:19 (NJB)

She [wisdom] is more precious than jewels; and nothing you desire compares with her. Proverbs 3:15 (CEV)

What evil people dread most will happen to them, but good people will get what they want most. Proverbs 10:24 (CEV)

The sluggard craves and gets nothing, but the desires of the diligent are fully satisfied. Proverbs 13:4 (NIV)

What matters most is loyalty. It is better to be poor than to be a liar. Proverbs 19:22 (CEV)

I belong to my love, and his desire is for me. Song of Songs 7:10 (NJB)

For I desire steadfast love and not sacrifice, the knowledge of God rather than burnt offerings. Hosea 6:6 (NRSV)

And the worries of the world, and the deceitfulness of riches, and the desires for other things enter in and choke the word, and it becomes unfruitful. Mark 4:19 (NASB)

Therefore consider the members of your earthly body as dead to immorality, impurity, passion, evil desire, and greed, which amounts to idolatry. Colossians 3:5 (NASB)

Run from temptations that capture young people. Always do the right thing. Be faithful, loving, and easy to get along with. Worship with people whose hearts are pure. 2 Timothy 2:22 (CEV)

Then, after desire has conceived, it gives birth to sin; and sin, when it is full grown, gives birth to death. James 1:15 (NIV)

What causes fights and quarrels among you? Don't they come from your desires that battle within you? You want something but don't get it. You kill and covet, but you cannot have what you want. You quarrel and fight. You do not have, because you do not ask God.

When you ask, you do not receive, because you ask with wrong motives, that you may spend what you get on your pleasures. James 4:1–3 (NIV)

Behave like obedient children. Don't let your lives be controlled by your desires, as they used to be. 1 Peter 1:14 (CEV)

I urge you, my dear friends, as strangers and nomads, to keep yourself free from the disordered natural inclinations that attack the soul. 1 Peter 2:11 (NJB)

With their high-sounding but empty talk they tempt back people who have scarcely escaped from those who live in error, by playing

on the disordered desires of their human nature and by debaucheries. They may promise freedom but are themselves slaves to corruption; because if anyone lets himself be dominated by anything, then he is a slave to it. 2 Peter 2:18–19 (NJB)

Destiny
(*see also* THE FUTURE, GUIDANCE, *and* THE UNKNOWABLE)

And for all of us is reserved a common fate, for the upright and for the wicked, for the good and the bad; whether we are ritually pure or not, whether we offer sacrifice or not: it is the same for the good and for the sinner, for someone who takes a vow, as for someone who fears to do so. This is the evil in everything that happens under the sun: The same destiny overtakes all. Ecclesiastes 9:2–3 (NJB)

And we know that in all things God works for the good of those who love him, who have been called according to his purpose. Romans 8:28 (NIV)

Disappointment
(*see also* ACCEPTANCE *and* HOPE)

Sustain me according to your promise, and I will live; do not let my hopes be dashed. Psalms 119:116 (NIV)

. . . I am the Lord. You won't be disappointed if you trust in me. Isaiah 49:22–23 (CEV)

"You expected much, but see, it turned out to be little. What you brought home, I blew away. Why?" declares the Lord Almighty. "Because of my house, which remains a ruin, while each of you is busy with his own house." Haggai 1:9 (NIV)

Hope does not disappoint, because the love of God has been poured out within our hearts through the Holy Spirit who was given to us. Romans 5:5 (NASB)

Behold, I lay in Zion a stone of stumbling and a rock of offense, and he who believes in Him will not be disappointed. Romans 9:33 (TLB)

Doubt

(*see also* BELIEF, FAITHFUL-NESS, GUIDANCE, *and* HOPE)

And immediately Jesus stretched out His hand and took hold of him, and said to him, "O you of little faith, why did you doubt?" Matthew 14:31 (NASB)

And Jesus answered and said to them, "Truly I say to you, if you have faith, and do not doubt, you shall not only do what was done to the fig tree, but even if you say to this mountain, 'Be taken up and cast into the sea,' it shall happen." Matthew 21:21 (NASB)

I have faith. Help me overcome my lack of faith! Mark 9:24 (NJB)

Then saith he to Thomas, "Reach hither thy finger, and behold my hands; and reach hither thy hand and thrust it into my side: and be not faithless, but believing. And Thomas answered and said unto him, "My Lord and my God." Jesus saith unto him, "Thomas, because thou hast seen me, thou hast believed: blessed are they that have not seen, and yet have believed." John 20:27–29 (KJV)

Give a welcome to anyone whose faith is not strong, but do not get into arguments about doubtful points. Romans 14:1 (NJB)

But the prayer must be made with faith, and no trace of doubt, because a person who has doubts is like the waves thrown up in the sea by the buffeting of the wind. James 1:6 (NJB)

Be merciful to those who doubt; snatch others from the fire and save them; to others show mercy, mixed with fear—hating even the clothing stained by corrupted flesh. Jude 22–23 (NIV)

Dreams

(*see also* VISIONS)

And Jacob had a dream, and behold, a ladder was set on the earth with its top reaching to heaven; and behold, the angels of God were ascending and descending on it. Genesis 28:12 (NASB)

"We both had dreams," they answered, "but there is no one to interpret them." Then Joseph said to them, "Do not interpretations belong to God? Tell me your dreams." Genesis 40:8 (NJB)

He said, "Hear now My words: If there is a prophet among you, I, the Lord, shall make Myself known to him in a vision. I shall speak with him in a dream." Numbers 12:6 (NASB)

In a dream, in a vision of the night, when deep sleep falls on men as they slumber in their beds, he may speak in their ears and terrify them with warnings . . . to preserve his soul from the pit, his life from perishing by the sword. Job 33:15–18 (NIV)

Like a dream when one awakes, O Lord, when aroused, Thou wilt despise their form. Psalms 73:20 (NASB)

For in many dreams and in many words there is emptiness. Rather, fear God. Ecclesiastes 5:7 (NASB)

Their dreams and my truth are as different as straw and

wheat. But when prophets speak for me, they must say only what I have told them. Jeremiah 23:28 (CEV)

There is a God in heaven who reveals mysteries. Daniel 2:28 (NASB)

I had a dream, it appalled me. Dread assailed me as I lay in bed; the visions that passed through my head tormented me. Daniel 4:5 (NJB)

The angel of the Lord appeared to him in a dream. Matthew 1:20 (KJV)

I have suffered many things this day in a

dream because of him. Matthew 27:19 (KJV)

Your young men shall see visions, and your old men shall dream dreams. Acts 2:17 (NRSV)

Duty
(*see also* GOALS *and* RESPONSIBILITY)

Teach them the decrees and laws, and show them the way to live and the duties they are to perform. Exodus 18:20 (NIV)

The people all responded together,

"We will do everything the Lord has said." So Moses brought their answer back to the Lord. Exodus 19:8 (NASB)

Everything you were taught can be put into a few words: Respect and obey God! This is what life is all about. Ecclesiastes 12:13 (CEV)

Even the stork in the sky knows her seasons; and the turtledove and the swift and the thrush observe the time of their migration; but my people do not know the ordinance of the Lord. Jeremiah 8:7 (NASB)

You have already been told what is right and what the Lord wants of you. Only this, to do what is right, to love loyalty and to walk humbly with your God. Micah 6:8 (NJB)

Be on guard for yourselves and for all the flock, among which the Holy Spirit has made you overseers, to shepherd the church of God which He purchased with His own blood. Acts 20:28 (NASB)

Let the husband fulfill his duty to his wife, and likewise also the wife to her husband. 1 Corinthians 7:3 (NASB)

As a prisoner of the Lord, then, I beg you to live a life that is worthy of the people God has chosen to be his own. Ephesians 4:1 (CEV)

Pay to all what is due then—taxes to whom taxes are due, revenue to whom revenue is due, respect to whom respect is due, honor to whom honor is due. Romans 13:7 (NRSV)

Education

(*see also* LEARNING *and* WISDOM)

The fear of the Lord is the beginning of knowledge; fools despise wisdom and instruction. Proverbs 1:7 (NASB)

Hold firmly to my teaching and never let go. It will mean life for you. Proverbs 4:13 (CEV)

Take my instruction, and not silver, and knowledge rather than choicest gold. Proverbs 8:10 (NASB)

Teach your children right from wrong, and when they are grown they will still do right. Proverbs 22:6 (CEV)

Be warned, my son, of anything in addition to them. Of making many books there is no end, and much study wearies the body. Ecclesiastes 12:12 (NIV)

The Jews therefore were marveling, saying, "How has this man become learned, having never been educated?" John 7:15 (NASB)

I am a Jew, born in Tarsus of Cilicia, but brought up in this city, educated under Gamaliel, strictly according to the law of our fathers, being zealous for God, just as you all are today. Acts 22:3 (NASB)

Knowledge makes us proud of ourselves, while love makes us helpful to others. 1 Corinthians 8:1 (CEV)

See to it that no one takes you captive through philosophy and empty deception, according to the tradition of men, according to the elementary principles of the world, rather than according to Christ. Colossians 2:8 (NASB)

Employment
(see also SELF-SUFFICIENCY and WORK ETHIC)

Six days you shall labor and do all your work. Exodus 20:9 (NRSV)

Do not take advantage of a hired man who is poor and needy, whether he is a brother Israelite or an alien living in one of your towns. Deuteronomy 24:14 (NIV)

But as for you, be strong and do not give up, for your work will be rewarded. 2 Chronicles 15:7 (NIV)

A slack hand brings poverty, but the hand of the diligent brings wealth. Proverbs 10:4 (KJV)

Abundance of good things is the fruit of the lips; labor brings its own return. Proverbs 12:14 (KJV)

Do you see a man skilled in his work? He will stand before kings; He will not stand before obscure men. Proverbs 22:29 (NASB)

Come to me, all you who are weary and burdened, and I will give you rest. Matthew 11:28 (NIV)

Then some soldiers asked him, "And what should we do?" He replied, "Don't extort money and don't accuse people falsely—be content with your pay." Luke 3:14 (NIV)

The laborer is worthy of his wages. Luke 10:7 (KJV)

Each will receive wages according to the labor of each. 1 Corinthians 3:8 (KJV)

Thieves must give up stealing; rather let them labor and work honestly with their own hands, so as to have something to share with the needy. Ephesians 4:28 (NRSV)

Make every effort to present yourself before God as a proven worker who has no need to be ashamed, but who keeps the message of truth on a straight path. 2 Timothy 2:15 (NJB)

Energy

(*see also* ACTION, FATIGUE, PERSEVERANCE, *and* PRODUCTIVITY)

And for this purpose also I labor, striving according to His power, which mightily works within me. Colossians 1:29 (NASB)

Whatever you do, work at it with all your heart, as working for the Lord, not for men, since you know that you will receive an inheritance from the Lord as a reward. It is the Lord Christ you are serving. Colossians 3:23–4 (NIV)

Reaping at harvest-time is the mark of the prudent, sleeping at harvest-time is the sign of the worthless. Proverbs 10:5 (NJB)

Idleness lulls to sleep, the feckless soul will go hungry. Ecclesiastes 10:18 (NJB)

Therefore, my dear brothers, stand firm. Let nothing move you. Always give yourselves fully to the work of the Lord, because you know that your labor in the Lord is not in vain. 1 Corinthians 15:58 (NIV)

Environment

(*see also* NATURE)

. . . let them have dominion over the fish of the sea, and over the birds of the air, and

45

over the cattle, and over all the wild animals of the earth, and over every creeping thing that creeps upon the earth. Genesis 1:26 (NRSV)

When you besiege a city a long time, to make war against it in order to capture it, you shall not destroy its trees by swinging an axe against them; for you may eat from them, and you shall not cut them down. For is the tree of the field a man, that it should be besieged by you? Deuteronomy 20:19 (NASB)

Do not pollute the land where you are. Bloodshed pollutes the land, and atonement cannot be made for the land on which blood has been shed, except by the blood of the one who shed it. Numbers 35:33 (NIV)

And he went out to the spring of water, and threw salt in it and said, "Thus says the Lord, 'I have purified these waters; there shall not be from there death or unfruitfulness any longer.' " 2 Kings 2:21 (NASB)

For you will have a covenant with the stones of the field, and the wild animals will be at peace with you. Job 5:23 (NIV)

But ask the animals, and they will teach you, or the birds of the air, and they will tell you; or speak to the earth, and it will teach you, or let the fish of the sea inform you. Job 12:7 (NIV)

The earth is the Lord's, and all it contains, the world, and those who dwell in it. Psalms 24:1 (NASB)

He loves righteousness and justice; the earth is full of the lovingkindness of the Lord. Psalms 33:5 (NASB)

O Lord, how many are Thy works! In wisdom Thou hast made them all; the earth is full of Thy possessions. Psalms 104:24 (NASB)

The highest heavens belong to the Lord, but the earth he has given to man. Psalms 115:16 (NIV)

There is a time for everything, and a season for every activity under heaven. Ecclesiastes 3:1 (NIV)

The land mourns and wastes away, Lebanon is ashamed and withers; Sharon is like the Arabah, and Bashan and Carmel drop their leaves. Isaiah 33:9 (NIV)

For this is what the Lord says—he who created the heavens, he is God; he who fashioned and made the earth, he founded it; he did not create it to be empty, but formed it to be inhabited—he says: "I am the Lord, and there is no other." Isaiah 45:18 (NIV)

Faithfulness

(*see also* BELIEF, DOUBT, *and* HOPE)

O love the Lord, all you His saints: for the Lord preserveth the faithful, and plentifully rewardeth the proud doer. Psalms 31:23 (KJV)

I will sing of the Lord's great love forever; with my mouth I will make your faithfulness known through all generations. Psalms 89:1 (NIV)

The faithless will be fully repaid for their ways, and the good man rewarded for his. Proverbs 14:14 (NIV)

Many describe themselves as people of faithful love, but who can find someone really to be trusted? Proverbs 20:6 (NJB)

I believe; help my unbelief. Mark 9:24 (NRSV)

For by grace you have been saved through faith, and this is not your own doing; it is the gift of God—not the result of works, so that no one may boast. Romans 2:8–9 (NRSV)

We conclude that a man is justified by faith without the deeds of the law. Romans 3:28 (KJV)

Being justified by faith, we have peace with God through our Lord

Jesus Christ. Romans 5:1 (KJV)

I have fought the good fight, I have finished the race, I have kept the faith. 2 Timothy 4:7 (NIV)

To those who are pure themselves, everything is pure; to those who have been corrupted and lack faith, nothing can be pure—the corruption is both in their minds and their consciences. Titus 1:15 (NJB)

Resist him, standing firm in the faith, because you know that your brothers throughout the world are undergoing the same kind of sufferings. 1 Peter 5:9 (NIV)

Keep faithful, and I will give you the crown of life for your prize. Revelation 2:10 (NJB)

Family

(*see also* CHILDREN *and* PARENTING)

In you all the families of the earth shall be blessed. Genesis 12:3 (NRSV)

Then King David went in and sat before the Lord, and he said:

"Who am I, O Lord God, and what is my family, that you have brought me this far?" 1 Chronicles 17:16 (NIV)

Jahath was the eldest, Zizah the second, then Jeush and Beriah, who had not many children and were reckoned as one family. 1 Chronicles 23:11 (NJB)

For what does he care about the family he leaves behind when his allotted months come to an end? Job 21:21 (NIV)

He who troubles his own house will inherit wind, and the foolish will be servant to the wisehearted. Proverbs 11:29 (NASB)

Your brothers, your own family—even they have betrayed you; they have raised a loud cry against you. Do not trust them, though they speak well of you. Jeremiah 12:6 (NIV)

Here are my mother and my brothers! For whoever does the will of my Father in heaven is my brother and sister and mother. Matthew 12:49–50 (NRSV)

So then you are no longer strangers and aliens, but you are citizens with the saints and also the household of God. Ephesians 2:19 (NRSV)

Here is a trustworthy saying: If anyone sets his heart on being an overseer, he desires a noble task . . . He must manage his own family well

and see that his children obey him with proper respect. 1 Timothy 3:1–4 (NIV)

How can any man who does not understand how to manage his own household take care of the Church of God? 1 Timothy 3:5 (NJB)

A deacon must be the husband of but one wife and must manage his children and his household well. 1 Timothy 3:12 (NIV)

But if any widow has children or grandchildren, let them first learn to practice piety in regard to their own family, and to make some return to their parents; for this is acceptable in the sight of God. 1 Timothy 5:4 (NASB)

But if anyone does not provide for his own, and especially for those of his household, he has denied the faith, and is worse than an unbeliever. 1 Timothy 5:8 (NASB)

I have been reminded of your sincere faith, which first lived in your grandmother Lois and your mother Eunice and, I am persuaded, now lives in you. 2 Timothy 1:5 (NIV)

Both the one who makes men holy and those who are made holy are of the same family. So Jesus is not ashamed to call them brothers. Hebrews 2:11 (NIV)

By faith Noah, when warned about things not yet seen, in holy fear built an ark to save

his family. Hebrews 11:7 (NIV)

Fatigue
(*see also* ACTION *and* ENERGY)

When Moses' hands grew tired, they took a stone and put it under him and he sat on it. Aaron and Hur held his hands up—one on one side, one on the other—so that his hands remained steady till sunset. Exodus 17:12 (NIV)

Not one of them grows tired or stumbles, not one slumbers or sleeps; not a belt is loosened at the waist, not a sandal thong is broken. Isaiah 5:27 (NIV)

Do you not know? Have you not heard? The Everlasting God, the Lord, the Creator of the ends of the earth Does not become weary or tired. His understanding is inscrutable. Isaiah 40:28 (NASB)

Though youths grow weary and tired, and vigorous young men stumble badly, yet those who wait for the Lord will gain new strength; They will mount up with wings like eagles, they will run and not get tired, they will walk and not become weary. Isaiah 40:30–31 (NASB)

No discipline seems pleasant at the time, but painful.

Later on, however, it produces a harvest of righteousness and peace for those who have been trained by it. Therefore, strengthen your feeble arms and weak knees. Hebrews 12:11-12 (NIV)

Faults

(*see also* ACCEPTANCE, BLAME, FORGIVENESS, JUDGMENT, *and* MERCY)

I am pure and without sin; I am clean and free from guilt. Yet God has found fault with me; he considers me his enemy. Job 33:9 (NIV)

But who can detect their errors? Clear me from hidden faults. Psalms 19:12 (NRSV)

Through your own fault you will lose the inheritance I gave you. I will enslave you to your enemies in a land you do not know, for you have kindled my anger, and it will burn forever. Jeremiah 17:4 (NIV)

"Pick me up and throw me into the sea," he replied, "and it will become calm. I know that it is my fault that this great storm has come upon you." Jonah 1:12 (NIV)

If your brother sins against you, go and show him his fault, just between the two of you. If he listens to you, you have won your brother over. Matthew 18:15 (NIV)

Why do you see the speck in your neighbor's eye, but not notice the log in your own eye? Or how you say to your neighbor, "Friend, let me take out the speck in your eye," when you yourself do not see the log in your own eye? You hypocrite, first take the log out of your own eye, and then you will see clearly to take the speck out of your neighbor's eye. Luke 6:41–42 (NRSV)

If any of you lacks wisdom, he should ask God, who gives generously to all without finding fault, and it will be given to him. James 1:5 (NIV)

For whoever keeps the whole law and yet stumbles at just one point is guilty of breaking all of it. James 2:10 (NIV)

We all trip up in many ways. Someone who does not trip up in speech has reached perfection and is able to keep the whole body in tight reign. James 3:2 (NJB)

Confess your faults one to another, and pray one for another, that ye may be healed. James 5:16 (KJV)

Fear

(see also ANXIETY, COURAGE, FAITHFULNESS, HOPE, PROTECTION, and SECURITY)

Fear of God (Reverence)

"Do not lay a hand on the boy," he said. "Do not do

54

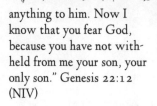

anything to him. Now I know that you fear God, because you have not withheld from me your son, your only son." Genesis 22:12 (NIV)

Oh that they had such a heart in them, that they would fear Me, and keep all My commandments always, that it may be well with them and with their sons forever! Deuteronomy 5:29 (NASB)

Fear the Lord your God, serve him only and take your oaths in his name. Deuteronomy 6:13 (NIV)

Now then let the fear of the Lord be upon you; be very careful what you do, for the Lord our God will have no part in unrighteousness, or partiality, or the taking of a bribe. 2 Chronicles 19:7 (NASB)

You who fear the Lord, trust in the Lord; He is their help and their shield. Psalms 115:11 (NASB)

Who among you fears the Lord and obeys the word of his servant? Let him who walks in the dark, who has no light, trust in the name of the Lord and rely on his God. Isaiah 50:10 (NIV)

And a voice came from the throne, saying, "Give praise to our God, all you His bond-servants, you who fear Him, the small and the great." Revelation 19:5 (NASB)

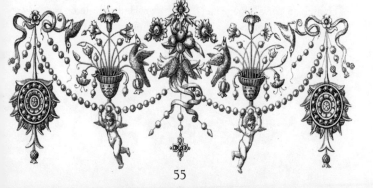

Fear (In General)

Then even the bravest soldier, whose heart is like the heart of a lion, will melt with fear, for all Israel knows that your father is a fighter and that those with him are brave. 2 Samuel 17:10 (NIV)

The arrows of the Almighty are in me, my spirit drinks in their poison; God's terrors are marshaled against me. Job 6:4 (NIV)

Yea, thou I walk through the valley of the shadow of death, I will fear no evil: for thou art with me; thy rod and thy staff they comfort me. Psalms 23:4 (KJV)

Though an army besiege me, my heart will not fear;

though war break out against me, even then will I be confident. Psalms 27:3 (NIV)

I sought the Lord, and he heard me, and delivered me from all my fears. Psalms 34:4 (NRSV)

The fear of man brings a snare, but he who trusts in the Lord will be exalted. Proverbs 29:25 (NASB)

Say to those with anxious heart, "take courage, fear not. Behold, your God will come with vengence; the recompense of God will come, But He will save you." Isaiah 35:4 (NASB)

But I will warn you whom to fear: fear the One who after He has killed has authority to cast into hell;

yes, I tell you, fear Him!
Luke 12:5 (NASB)

Pray also for me, that whenever I open my mouth, words
may be given me so that I will
fearlessly make known the
mystery of the gospel for
which I am an ambassador in
chains. Pray that I may declare
it fearlessly, as I should. Ephesians 6:19–20 (NIV)

There is no fear in love; but
perfect love casts out fear,
because fear involves punishment, and the one who fears
is not perfected in love.
1 John 4:18 (NASB)

Forgiveness
(*see also* ANGER, BLAME,
FAULTS, MERCY, *and* SIN)

But He, being compas-
sionate, forgave their iniquity, and did not destroy
them; and often He
restrained His anger, and did
not arouse all His wrath.
Thus He remembered that
they were but flesh, a wind
that passes and does not
return. Psalms 78:38–39
(NASB)

"Come now, let us reason
together," says the Lord.
"Though your sins are like
scarlet, they shall be as
white as snow; though they
are red as crimson, they shall
be like wool." Isaiah 1:18
(NIV)

Forgive us our debts, as we also have forgiven our debtors. Matthew 6:12 (NRSV)

For if you forgive men for their transgressions, your heavenly Father will also forgive you. But if you do not forgive men, then your Father will not forgive your transgressions. Matthew 6:14–15 (NASB)

And behold, they were bringing to Him a paralytic, lying on a bed; and Jesus seeing their faith said to the paralytic, "Take courage, My son, your sins are forgiven." Matthew 9:2 (NASB)

The Son of Man has the authority on earth to forgive sins. Matthew 9:6 (NRSV)

"Lord, if another member of the church sins against me, how often should I forgive? As many as seven times?" Jesus said to him, "Not seven times, I tell you, but seventy times seven." Matthew 18:21–22 (NRSV)

Be on your guard! If your brother sins, rebuke him; and if he repents, forgive him. Luke 17:3 (NASB)

Jesus said, "Father, forgive them, for they do not know what they are doing." Luke 23:34 (NIV)

All the prophets testify about Him that everyone who believes in Him receives forgiveness of sins through His name. Acts 10:43 (NIV)

In your anger do not sin: Do not let the sun go down while you are still angry, and do not give the devil a foothold. Ephesians 4:26–27 (NIV)

And be kind to one another, tender-hearted, forgiving each other, just as God in Christ also has forgiven you. Ephesians 4:32 (NASB)

For He has rescued us from the dominion of darkness and brought us into the kingdom of the Son He loves, in whom we have redemption, the forgiveness of sins. Colossians 1:13–14 (NIV)

Just as the Lord has forgiven you, so must you also forgive. Colossians 3:13 (NRSV)

And according to the Law, one may almost say, all things are cleansed with blood, and without shedding of blood there is no forgiveness. Hebrews 9:22 (NASB)

I am writing to you, little children, because your sins are forgiven you for His name's sake. 1 John 2:12 (NASB)

Freedom

Thus saith the Lord God of Israel, Let My People go. Exodus 5:1 (KJV)

Proclaim liberty throughout all the land unto all inhabitants thereof. Leviticus 25:10 (KJV)

And you shall know the truth, and the truth shall make you free. John 8:32 (NASB)

If the son therefore shall make you free, ye shall be free indeed. John 8:36 (KJV)

For freedom Christ has set us free. Stand firm therefore and do not submit again to a yoke of slavery. Galatians 5:1 (NRSV)

For he who was a slave when he was called by the Lord is the Lord's freed man; similarly, he who was a free man when he was called is

Christ's slave. 1 Corinthians 7:22 (NIV)

You were bought with a price; do not become slaves of men. 1 Corinthians 7:23 (NIV)

Now the Lord is the Spirit; and where the Spirit of the Lord is, there is liberty. 2 Corinthians 3:17 (NASB)

After all, brothers, you were called to be free; do not use your freedom as an opening for self-indulgence, but be servants to one another in love. Galatians 5:13 (NJB)

They promise them freedom, while they themselves are slaves of

depravity—for a man is a slave to whatever has mastered him.
2 Peter 2:19 (NIV)

Friendship

(*see also* COMPAN-IONSHIP *and* RELATIONSHIPS)

Jonathan said to David, "Go in peace, for we have sworn friendship with each other in the name of the Lord, saying, 'The Lord is witness between you and me, and between your descendants and my descendants forever.'" Then David left, and Jonathan went back to the town.
1 Samuel 20:42 (NIV)

This is My command-ment, that you love one another, just as I have loved you. Greater love has no more than this, that one lay down his life for his friends. You are My friends, if you do what I command you. No longer do I call you slaves, for the slave does not know what his master is doing; but I have called you friends, for all things that I have heard from My Father I have made known to you. John 15:12-15 (NASB)

Fulfillment

(*see also* GOALS, REWARDS, SUCCESS, *and* VICTORY)

For He has satisfied the thirsty soul, and the hungry soul He has filled with what is good. Psalms 107:9 (NASB)

A longing fulfilled is sweet to the soul, but fools detest turning from evil. Proverbs 13:19 (NIV)

Do not think that I have come to abolish the Law or the Prophets; I have not come to abolish them but to fulfill them. Matthew 5:17 (NIV)

All the law is fulfilled in one word, even in this; Thou shalt love thy neighbor as thyself. Galatians 5:14 (KJV)

Bear one another's burdens, and in this you will fulfill the law of Christ. Galatians 6:2 (NRSV)

And you have been given fullness in Christ, who is the head over every power and authority. Colossians 2:10 (NIV)

You say, "I am rich; I have acquired wealth and do not need a thing." But you do not realize that you are wretched, pitiful, poor, blind and naked. Revelation 3:17 (NIV)

The Future

(*see also* THE PRESENT, TIME, TOMORROW, *and* THE UNKNOWABLE)

Have you not heard that I determined it long ago? I planned from days of old what now I bring to pass. 2 Kings 19:25 (NRSV)

Do not boast about tomorrow, for you do not know what a day may bring forth. Proverbs 27:1 (NIV)

Therefore do not worry about tomorrow, for tomorrow will worry about itself. Each day has enough trouble of its own. Matthew 6:34 (NIV)

He said to them: "It is not for you to know the times or dates the Father has set by his own authority." Acts 1:7 (NIV)

Known unto God are all His works from the beginning of the world. Acts 15:18 (KJV)

For you yourselves know that the day of the Lord will come like a thief in the night. 1 Thessalonians 5:2 (NRSV)

Why, you do not even know what will happen tomorrow. What is your life? You are a mist that appears for a little while and then vanishes. James 4:14 (NIV)

Then he told me, "Do not seal up the words of the prophecy, because the time is near." Revelation 22:10 (NIV)

Generosity

(*see also* COMPASSION, FORGIVENESS, MERCY, *and* NEED)

You shall generously give to him, and your heart shall not be grieved when you give to him, because for this thing the Lord your God will bless you in all your work and in all your undertakings. Deuteronomy 15:10 (NASB)

All shall give as they are able according to the blessing of the Lord your God that he has given to you. Deuteronomy 16:17 (NRSV)

The wicked borrows and does not pay back, but the righteous is gracious and gives. Psalms 37:21 (NASB)

He has given freely to the poor; His righteousness endures forever; His horn will be exalted in honor. Psalms 112:9 (NASB)

The soul who blesses will prosper, whoever satisfies others will also be satisfied. Proverbs 11:25 (NJB)

A generous man will himself be blessed, for he shares his food with the poor. Proverbs 22:9 (NIV)

But when you give to the needy, do not let your left hand know what your right hand is doing. Matthew 6:3 (NIV)

Heal the sick, raise the dead, cleanse those who have leprosy, drive out demons. Freely you have received,

freely give. Matthew 10:8 (NIV)

Give to everyone who begs from you. Luke 6:30 (NRSV)

For all of them have contributed out of their abundance, but she out of her poverty has put in all she has had to live on. Luke 21:4 (NRSV)

In everything I showed you that by working hard in this manner you must help the weak and remember the words of the Lord Jesus, that He Himself said, "It is more blessed to give than to receive." Acts 20:35 (NASB)

Remember this: Whoever sows sparingly will also reap sparingly, and whoever sows generously will also reap generously. 2 Corinthians 9:6 (NIV)

Each one should give as much as he has decided on his own initiative, nor reluctantly or under compulsion, for God loves a cheerful giver. 2 Corinthians 9:7 (NJB)

Command them to do good, to be rich in good deeds, and to be generous and willing to share. 1 Timothy 6:18 (NIV)

God . . . gives to all generously and ungrudgingly. James 1:5 (NRSV)

65

Goals

(*see also* AMBITION *and* PERSEVERANCE)

Where there is no vision, the people perish: but he that keepeth the law, happy is he. Proverbs 29:18 (KJV)

Better is the end of a thing than its beginning. Ecclesiastes 7:8 (NRSV)

At the time I have decided my words will come true. You can trust what I say about the future. It may take a long time, but keep on waiting—it will come true! Habakkuk 2:3 (CEV)

Everyone who asks receives; everyone who searches finds; who knocks will have the door opened. Matthew 7:8 (NJB)

The one who endures to the end will be saved. Matthew 10:22 (NRSV)

If you believe, you will receive whatever you ask for in prayer. Matthew 21:22 (NIV)

Now he who plants and he who waters are one; but each will receive his own reward according to his own labor. 1 Corinthians 3:8 (NASB)

What we aim for is not visible but invisible. Visible things are transitory, but invisible things eternal. 2 Corinthians 4:18 (NJB)

I press toward the mark for the prize of the high calling of God in Christ Jesus. Philippians 3:14 (KJV)

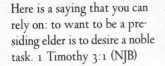

Here is a saying that you can rely on: to want to be a presiding elder is to desire a noble task. 1 Timothy 3:1 (NJB)

I have fought the good fight, I have finished the race, I have kept the faith. 2 Timothy 4:7 (NRSV)

God's Will

It is the Lord: let Him do what seemeth to Him good. 1 Samuel 3:18 (KJV)

And all the inhabitants of the earth are accounted as nothing, but He does according to His will in the host of heaven and among the inhabitants of earth; and

no one can ward off His hand or say to Him, "What hast Thou done?" Daniel 4:35 (NASB)

Do not be conformed to this world, but be transformed by the renewing of your minds so that you may discern what is the will of God—what is good and acceptable and perfect. Psalms 12:2 (NRSV)

Not everyone who says to me, "Lord, Lord" will enter the kingdom of heaven, but only the one who does the will of my Father in heaven. Matthew 7:21 (NRSV)

Our Father, which art in heaven, hallowed be Thy name. Thy kingdom come. Thy will be done on earth,

as it is in heaven. Matthew 6:9–10 (KJV)

Father, if Thou art willing, remove this cup from Me; yet not My will, but Thine be done. Luke 22:42 (NASB)

I can do nothing on My own initiative. As I hear, I judge; and My judgment is just, because I do not seek My own will, but the will of Him who sent Me. John 5:30 (NASB)

And this is the will of Him who sent Me, that of all that He has given Me I lose nothing, but raise it up on the last day. John 6:39 (NASB)

Also we have obtained an inheritance, having been predestined according to His purpose who works all things after the counsel of His will, to the end that we who were the first to hope in Christ should be to the praise of His glory. Ephesians 1:11–12 (NASB)

It is God's will that you should be sanctified: that you should avoid sexual immorality; that each of you should learn to control his own body in a way that is holy and honorable. 1 Thessalonians 4:3–4 (NIV)

This is good, and pleases God our Savior, who wants all people to be saved and to come to a knowledge of the truth. 1 Timothy 2:3–4 (GNB)

Ye ought to say, "If the Lord will, we shall live, and do this, or that." James 4:15 (KJV)

And the world is passing away, and also its lusts; but the one who does the will of God abides forever. 1 John 2:17 (NASB)

Worthy art Thou, our Lord and our God, to receive glory and honor and power; for Thou didst create all things, and because of Thy will they existed, and were created. Revelation 4:11 (NASB)

Goodness
(*see also* GREATNESS, RIGHTEOUSNESS, *and* VIRTUE)

And God saw that the light was good; and God separated the light from the darkness. Genesis 1:4 (NASB)

And God saw all that He had made, and behold, it was very good. And there was evening and there was

morning, the sixth day. Genesis 1:31 (NASB)

Lo, God will not reject a man of integrity, nor will He support the evildoers. Job 8:20 (NASB)

Surely goodness and mercy shall follow me all the days of my life. Psalms 23:6 (KJV)

Trust in the Lord and do good; dwell in the land and enjoy safe pasture. Psalms 37:3 (NIV)

For the Lord is good and his love endures forever; his faithfulness continues through all generations. Psalms 100:5 (NASB)

O give thanks to the Lord, for he is good; for his stead-fast love endures forever. Psalms 106:1 (NRSV)

Refuse no kindness to those who have a right to it, if it is in your power to perform it. Proverbs 3:27 (NJB)

Seek good, not evil, that you may live. Then the Lord God Almighty will be with you, just as you say he is. Amos 5:14 (NIV)

His master replied, "Well done, good and faithful servant! You have been faithful with a few things; I will put you in charge of many things. Come and share your master's happiness!" Matthew 25:21 (NIV)

And Jesus said to him, "Why do you call Me good? No one is good except

God alone." Mark 10:18 (NASB)

Finally, brethren, whatever is true, whatever is honorable, whatever is right, whatever is pure, whatever is lovely, whatever is of good repute, if there is any excellence and if anything worthy of praise, let your mind dwell on these things. Philippians 4:8 (NIV)

Beloved, do not imitate what is evil, but what is good. The one who does good is of God; the one who does evil has not seen God. 3 John 11 (NASB)

Gratitude
(*see also* BLESSINGS, PRAISING GOD, *and* WORSHIP)

I will praise the name of God with a song, and will magnify Him with thanksgiving. Psalms 69:30 (KJV)

O give thanks to the Lord, for he is good; for his steadfast love endures forever. Psalms 106:1 (NRSV)

How good it is to sing praises to our God. Psalms 147:1 (NRSV)

Coming up to them at that very moment, she gave thanks to God and spoke about the child to all who were looking forward to the redemption of Jerusalem. Luke 2:38 (NIV)

Now one of them, when he saw that he had been healed, turned back, glorifying God with a loud voice, and he fell on his face at His feet, giving thanks to Him. And he was a Samaritan. Luke 17:15–16 (NASB)

Nor should there be obscenity, foolish talk or coarse joking, which are out of place, but rather thanksgiving. Ephesians 5:4 (NIV)

Do not be anxious about anything, but in everything, by prayer and petition, with thanksgiving, present your requests to God. Philippians 4:6 (NIV)

And for all things give thanks; this is the will of God for you in Jesus Christ. 1 Thessalonians 5:18 (NJB)

I always thank my God as I remember you in my prayers, because I hear about your faith in the Lord Jesus and your love for all the saints. Philemon 4–5 (NIV)

Thanks be to God for his indescribable gift! 2 Corinthians 9:15 (NIV)

Greatness
(*see also* GOODNESS, RIGHTEOUSNESS, *and* VIRTUE)

I know that the Lord is greater than all Gods. Exodus 18:11 (NIV)

Thine, O God, is the greatness, and the power, and the glory, and the victory, and the majesty. 1 Chronicles 29:11 (NIV)

God is greater than man. Job 33:12 (NIV)

Anyone who breaks one of the least of these commandments and teaches others to do the same will be called least in the kingdom of heaven, but whoever practices and teaches these commands will be called great in the kingdom of heaven. Matthew 5:19 (NIV)

Whoever becomes humble like this child is the greatest in the kingdom of heaven. Matthew 18:4 (NRSV)

You know that the rules of the gentiles lord it over them, and their great ones are tyrants over them. It will not be so among you; but whoever wishes to be great among you must first be your servant, and whoever wishes to be first among you must be your slave. Matthew 20:25–26 (NRSV)

And he was preaching, and saying, "After me One is coming who is mightier than I, and I am not fit to stoop down and untie the thong of His sandals." Mark 1:7 (NASB)

Whoever receives this child in My name receives Me; and whoever receives Me receives Him who sent Me; for he who is least among you, this is the one who is great. Luke 9:48 (NASB)

Remember the word that I said to you, "A slave is not greater than his master." If they persecuted Me, they will also persecute you; if they kept My word, they will keep yours also. John 15:20 (NASB)

Great and marvelous are thy works, Lord God Almighty. Revelation 15:3 (NIV)

Grief
(*see also* DEATH, HOPE, *and* SUFFERING)

And the king was deeply moved and went up to the chamber over the gate and wept. And thus he said as he walked, "O my son Absalom, my son, my son Absalom! Would I had died instead of you, O Absalom, my son, my son!" 2 Samuel 18:33 (NASB)

The Lord is near to the brokenhearted, and saves those who are crushed in spirit. Psalms 34:18 (NASB)

Out of the depths I cry to you, O Lord. Psalms 130:1 (NRSV)

By the waters of Babylon, there we sat down, yea, we wept, when we remembered Zion. Psalms 137:1 (KJV)

In much wisdom is much grief. Ecclesiastes 1:18 (KJV)

A time to weep, and a time to laugh; a time to mourn,

and a time to dance. Ecclesiastes 3:4 (NASB)

Keep your voice from weeping and your eyes from tears. Jeremiah 31:16 (NRSV)

And your turbans will be on your heads and your shoes on your feet. You will not mourn, and you will not weep; but you will rot away in your iniquities, and you will groan to one another. Ezekiel 24:21–23 (NASB)

Jesus turned and said to them, "Daughters of Jerusalem, do not weep for me; weep for yourselves and for your children." Luke 23:28 (NASB)

Blessed are those who mourn, for they shall be comforted. Matthew 5:4 (NIV)

Truly, truly, I say to you, that you will weep and lament, but the world will rejoice; you will be sorrowful, but your sorrow will be turned to joy. John 16:20 (NASB)

He will wipe every tear from their eyes. Death will be no more; mourning and crying and pain will be no more, for the first things have passed away. Revelation 21:4 (NRSV)

Guidance
(*see also* GOD'S WILL)

Make me know Thy ways, O Lord; Teach me Thy path. Psalms 25:4 (NASB)

He guides the humble in what is right and teaches them his way. Psalms 25:9 (NIV)

The steps of a man are established by the Lord; and He delights in his way. Psalms 37:23 (NASB)

For such is God, Our God forever and ever; He will guide us until death. Psalms 48:14 (NASB)

Teach me your way, O Lord, and I will walk in your truth; give me an undivided heart, that I may fear your name. Psalms 86:11 (NIV)

Your word is a lamp to my feet and a light to my path. Psalms 119:105 (NRSV)

The sun will no more be your light by day, nor will the brightness of the moon shine on you, for the Lord will be your everlasting light, and your God will be your glory. Isaiah 60:19 (NIV)

O Lord, correct me, but with judgment. Jeremiah 10:24 (KJV)

When I sit in darkness, the Lord shall be a light unto me. Micah 7:8 (KJV)

You are the light of the world. A city built on a hill cannot be hid. Matthew 5:14 (NRSV)

Jesus answered, "I am the way and the truth and the life. No one comes to the Father except through me." John 14:6 (NIV)

But when he, the Spirit of truth, comes, he will guide you into all truth. He will not speak on his own; he will speak only what he hears, and he will tell you what is yet to come. John 16:13 (NIV)

Haste
(*see also* PATIENCE)

But Thou, O Lord, be not far off; O Thou my help, hasten to my assistance. Psalms 22:19 (NASB)

Mastery of temper is high proof of intelligence, a quick temper makes folly worse ever. Proverbs 14:29 (NJB)

Where knowledge is wanting, zeal is not good; whoever goes too quickly stumbles. Proverbs 19:2 (NJB)

Do not be hasty in word or impulsive in thought to bring up a matter in the presence of God. For God is in heaven and you are on the earth; therefore let

your words be few. Ecclesiastes 5:2 (NASB)

But you will not leave in haste or go in flight; for the Lord will go before you, the God of Israel will be your rear guard. Isaiah 52:12 (NIV)

Healing
(*see also* FAITHFULNESS, HEALTH, HOPE, MIRACLES, *and* RECOVERY)

The Lord will keep you free from every disease. He will not inflict on you the horrible diseases you knew in Egypt, but he will inflict them on all who hate you. Deuteronomy 7:15 (NIV)

He maketh sore, and bindeth up: He woundeth, and His hands make whole. Job 5:18 (KJV)

Rash words are like sword thrusts, but the tongue of the wise brings healing. Proverbs 12:18 (NRSV)

A cheerful heart is good medicine, but a crushed spirit dries up the bones. Proverbs 17:22 (NIV)

But He was pierced for our transgressions, He was crushed for our iniquities; the punishment that brought us peace was upon Him, and by His wounds we are healed. Isaiah 53:5 (NIV)

Is there no balm in Gilead? Is there no physician there? Why then is there no

78

healing for the wound of my people? Jeremiah 8:22 (NIV)

Heal me, O Lord, and I will be healed; save me and I will be saved, for Thou art my praise. Jeremiah 17:14 (NASB)

Jesus said to them, "Surely you will quote this proverb to me: 'Physician, heal yourself! Do here in your hometown what we have heard that you did in Capernaum.'" Luke 4:23 (NIV)

And while the sun was setting, all who had any sick with various diseases brought them to Him; and laying His hands on every one of them, He was healing them. Luke 4:40 (NASB)

But that you may know that the Son of Man has authority on earth to forgive sins, He said to the paralyzed man, "I tell you, get up, take your mat and go home." Luke 5:24 (NIV)

So he replied to the messengers, "Go back and report to John what you have seen and heard: The blind receive sight, the lame walk, those who have leprosy are cured, the deaf hear, the dead are raised, and the good news is preached to the poor." Luke 7:22 (NIV)

Peter said to him, "Aeneas, Jesus Christ heals you; get up and make your bed!" Acts 9:34 (NRSV)

And the prayer offered in faith will make the sick person well; the Lord will

raise him up. If he has sinned, he will be forgiven. Therefore confess your sins to each other and pray for each other so that you may be healed. The prayer of a righteous man is powerful and effective. James 5:15–16 (NIV)

Health
(*see also* HEALING)

The Lord will turn away from you every illness. Deuteronomy 7:15 (NRSV)

The lord is the strength of my life. Psalms 27:1 (KJV)

A tranquil heart is life to the body, but passion is rotten-ness to the bones. Proverbs 14:30 (NASB)

A cheerful heart is good medicine, but a crushed spirit dries up the bones. Proverbs 17:22 (NIV)

A voice says, "Call out." Then he answered, "What shall I call out?" "All flesh is grass, and all its loveliness is like the flower of the field." Isaiah 40:6 (NASB)

Then your light shall break forth like the dawn, and your healing shall spring up quickly. Isaiah 58.8 (NRSV)

For I will restore health to you and your wounds I will heal. Jeremiah 30:17 (NRSV)

Or do you not know that your body is a temple of the

Holy Spirit who is in you, whom you have from God, and that you are not your own? For you have been bought with a price: therefore glorify God in your body. 1 Corinthians 6:19–20 (NASB)

Everyone who competes in the games goes into strict training. They do it to get a crown that will not last; but we do it to get a crown that will last forever. Therefore I do not run like a man running aimlessly; I do not fight like a man beating the air. No, I beat my body and make it my slave so that after I have preached to others, I myself will not be disqualified for the prize. 1 Corinthians 9:25–27 (NIV)

Heart

(*see also* DESIRE *and* LOVE)

You shall love the Lord your God will all your heart, and with all your soul, and with all your might. Deuteronomy 6:5 (NRSV)

Let the words of my mouth and the meditation of my heart be acceptance to you, O Lord, my rock and my redeemer. Psalms 19:14 (NRSV)

Create in me a clean heart, O God, and put a new and right spirit within me. Psalms 51:10 (NRSV)

My flesh and my heart may fail but God is the strength of my heart and my portion forever. Psalms 73:26 (NRSV)

Trust in the Lord with all your heart, and do not rely on your own insight. Proverbs 3:5 (NRSV)

Above all else, guard your heart, for it is the wellspring of life. Proverbs 4:23 (NIV)

A happy heart makes the face cheerful, but heartache crushes the spirit. Proverbs 15:13 (NIV)

For as he thinks within himself, so he is. He says to you, "Eat and drink!" But his heart is not with you. Proverbs 23:7 (NASB)

He hath sent me to bind up the broken-hearted. Isaiah 61:1 (KJV)

Blessed are the pure in heart for they will see God. Matthew 5:8 (NRSV)

And God, who searches the heart, knows what is the mind of the Spirit. Romans 8:27 (NRSV)

That if you confess with your mouth, "Jesus is Lord," and believe in your heart that God raised him from the dead, you will be saved. Romans 10:9 (NIV)

Holy Spirit
(*see also* FAITHFULNESS *and* MESSIAH)

And the earth was formless and void, and darkness was

over the surface of the deep; and the Spirit of God was moving over the surface of the waters. Genesis 1:2 (NASB)

The Spirit of the Lord shall rest upon him, the Spirit of wisdom and understanding, the Spirit of counsel and might, the Spirit of knowledge and of the fear of the Lord. Isaiah 11:2 (KJV)

The Spirit of the Sovereign Lord is on me, because the Lord has anointed me to preach good news to the poor. He has sent me to bind up the brokenhearted, to proclaim freedom for the captives and release from darkness for the prisoners. Isaiah 61:1 (NIV)

Here is my chosen servant! I love him, and he pleases me. I will give him my Spirit, and he will bring justice to the nations. Matthew 12:18 (CEV)

What is born of human nature is human; what is born of the Spirit is spirit. John 3:6 (NJB)

All of them were filled with the Holy Spirit and began to speak in other languages, as the Spirit gave them the ability. Acts 2:4 (NRSV)

No, this is what was spoken through the prophet Joel: "In the last days it will be, God declares, that I will pour out my Spirit upon all flesh." Acts 2:16-17 (NRSV)

In certain ways we are weak, but the Spirit is here to help us. For example, when we don't know what to pray for, the Spirit prays for us in ways that cannot be put into words. Romans 8:26 (CEV)

If we live with the Spirit, let us also walk in the Spirit. Galatians 5:25 (KJV)

Honesty
(*see also* TRUTH)

You shall not bear a false report; do not join your hand with a wicked man to be a malicious witness. Exodus 23:1 (NASB)

Keep thee far from a false matter. Exodus 23:7 (KJV)

You shall not steal, nor deal falsely, nor lie to one another. Leviticus 19:11 (NASB)

Nevertheless, the righteous will hold to their ways, and those with clean hands will grow stronger. Job 17:9 (NIV)

Better someone poor living an honest life than someone of devious ways, however rich. Proverbs 28:6 (NJB)

So then, putting away all falsehood, let all of us speak truth to our neighbors. Ephesians 4:25 (NRSV)

"These are the things that you must do. Speak the truth to one another; at your gates,

84

administer fair judgment conducive to death. Also let none of you devise evil in your heart against another, and do not love perjury; for all these are what I hate," declares the Lord. Zechariah 8:16–17 (NJB)

So from now on, there must be no more lies. Speak the truth to one another, since we are all parts of one another. Ephesians 4:25 (NJB)

But above all, my brethren, do not swear, either by heaven or by earth or with any other oath; but let your yes be yes, and your no, no; so that you may not fall under judgment. James 5:12 (NASB)

Whatever is true, whatever is honorable, whatever is just, whatever is pure, whatever is pleasing, whatever is commendable, if there is any excellence and if there is anything worthy of praise, think about these things. Philippians 4:8 (NRSV)

Hope

(see also BELIEF, COURAGE, and FAITHFULNESS)

For the needy will not always be forgotten, nor the hope of the afflicted perish forever. Psalms 9:18 (NASB)

For you have been my hope, O Sovereign Lord, my confi-

dence since my youth. Psalms 71:5 (NIV)

Out of the depths I have cried to Thee, O Lord.Lord, hear my voice! . . . If Thou, Lord, shouldst mark iniquities, O Lord, who could stand? But there is forgiveness with Thee, that Thou mayest be feared. I wait for the Lord, my soul does wait, and in His word do I hope. O Israel, hope in the Lord; for with the Lord there is lovingkindness, and with Him is abundant redemption. And He will redeem Israel from all his iniquities. Psalms 130 (NASB)

Hope deferred makes the heart sick, but desire fulfilled is a tree of life. Proverbs 13:12 (NASB)

Suffering produces endurance, endurance produces character, and character produces hope, and hope does not disappoint us, because God's love has been poured into our hearts through the Holy Spirit that has been given to us. Romans 5:3–5 (NRSV)

May the God of hope fill you with all joy and peace in believing, so that you may abound in hope by the power of the Holy Spirit. Romans 15:13 (NRSV)

If we have hoped in Christ in this life only, we are of all men most to be pitied. But now Christ has been raised from the dead, the first fruits of those who are asleep. 1 Corinthians 15:19–20 (NASB)

Hospitality
(*see also* GENEROSITY)

Anyone who receives a prophet because he is a prophet will receive a prophet's reward, and anyone who receives a righteous man because he is a righteous man will receive a righteous man's reward. Matthew 10:41 (NIV)

For I was hungry and you gave me something to eat, I was thirsty and you gave me something to drink, I was a stranger and you invited me in, I needed clothes and you clothed me, I was sick and you looked after me, I was in prison and you came to visit me. Matthew 25:35–36 (NIV)

Truly, truly, I say to you, he who receives whomever I send receives Me; and he who receives Me receives Him who sent Me. John 13:20 (NASB)

Extend hospitality to strangers. Romans 12:13 (NRSV)

Welcome one another, therefore, just as it has welcomed you for the glory of God. Romans 15:7 (NRSV)

Be not forgetful to entertain strangers: for thereby some have entertained angels unawares. Hebrews 13:2 (KJV)

Be hospitable to one another without complaint. 1 Peter 4:9 (NASB)

Humility

(see also CHARACTER, GRATITUDE, *and* SELF-IMAGE*)*

Who fed thee in the wilderness with manna, which thy fathers knew not, that he might humble thee, and that he might prove thee, to do thee good at thy latter end; and thou say in thine heart, "My power and the might of mine hand hath gotten me this wealth." Deuteronomy 8:16–17 (KJV)

My soul makes its boast in the Lord; let the humble hear and be glad. Psalms 34:2 (NRSV)

Too much pride causes trouble. Be sensible and take advice. Proverbs 13:10 (CEV)

This is what the Lord says: "Let not the wise man boast of his wisdom or the strong man boast of his strength or the rich man boast of his riches, but let him who boasts boast about this: that he understands and knows me, that I am the Lord, who exercises kindness, justice and righteousness on earth, for in these I delight," declares the Lord. Jeremiah 9:23–24 (NIV)

For whoever exalts himself will be hum-

bled, and whoever humbles himself will be exalted. Matthew 23:12 (NIV)

In the same way, younger people, be subject to the elders. Humility towards one another must be the garment you all wear constantly, because God opposes the proud but accords his favor to the humble. 1 Peter 5:5 (NJB)

Joy

(*see also* LAUGHTER *and* LOVE)

Then Hannah prayed and said, "my heart exults in the Lord; my horn is exalted in the Lord, my mouth speaks boldly against my enemies, because I rejoice in Thy salvation." 1 Samuel 2:1 (NASB)

The joy of the Lord is your strength. Nehemiah 8:10 (NRSV)

But let all who take refuge in Thee be glad, let them ever sing for joy; and mayest Thou shelter them, that those who love Thy name may exult in Thee. Psalms 5:11 (NASB)

For his anger lasts only a moment, but his favor lasts a lifetime; weeping may remain for a night, but rejoicing comes in the morning. Psalms 30:5 (NIV)

Be glad in the Lord and rejoice, you righteous ones, and shout for joy, all you who are upright in heart. Psalms 32:11 (NASB)

Clap your hands, all you nations; shout to God with cries of joy. Psalms 47:1 (NIV)

Let the nations be glad and sing for joy, for you judge the peoples with equity and guide the nations upon the earth. Psalms 67:4 (NRSV)

Those who sow in tears shall reap with joyful shouting. Psalms 126:5 (NASB)

With joy you will draw water from the wells of salvation. Isaiah 12:3 (NRSV)

For you shall go out in joy and be led back in peace; the mountains and the hills before you shall burst into song, and all the trees of the field clap their hands. Isaiah 55:12 (NRSV)

But the angel said to them, "Do not be afraid. I bring you good news of great joy that will be for all the people." Luke 2:10 (NIV)

I have said these things to you so that my joy may be in you, and that your joy may be complete. John 15:11 (NRSV)

90

May the God of hope fill you with all joy and peace in believing. Romans 15:13 (NRSV)

Rejoice in the Lord always; and again I will say, Rejoice. Philippians 4:4 (NRSV)

Whenever you face trials of any kind, consider it nothing but joy. James 1:2 (NRSV)

Judgment
(*see also* BLAME, JUSTICE, MERCY, *and* RESPONSIBILITY)

The Lord shall judge the ends of the earth. 1 Samuel 2:10 (KJV)

Teach me good judgment. Psalms 119:66 (KJV)

Open your mouth, judge righteously, and defend the rights of the afflicted and needy. Proverbs 31:9 (NASB)

Let judgment run down as waters, and righteousness as a mighty stream. Amos 5:24 (NRSV)

Do not judge lest you be judged. Matthew 7:1 (NASB)

And all the nations will be gathered before Him; and He will separate them from one another, as the shepherd separates the sheep from the goats; He will put the sheep on His right, and the goats on the left. Matthew 25:32–3 (NASB)

Do not judge by appearances, but judge by right judgment. John 7:24 (NRSV)

When they kept on questioning him, he straightened up and said to them, "If any one of you is without sin, let him be the first to throw a stone at her." John 8:7 (NIV)

You judge by human standards; I pass judgment on no one. John 8:15 (NIV)

Do not complain, brethren, against one another, that you yourselves may not be judged; behold, the Judge is standing right at the door. James 5:9 (NASB)

Justice
(*see also* JUDGMENT)

Surely, God will not act wickedly, and the Almighty will not pervert justice. Job 34:12 (NASB)

What does the Lord require of you, but to do justice, and to love kindness and to walk humbly with your God? Micah 6:8 (NRSV)

How long will you judge unjustly, And show partiality to the wicked? Psalms 82:2 (NASB)

Learn to do good; seek justice, reprove the ruthless; defend the orphan, plead for the widow. Isaiah 1:17 (NASB)

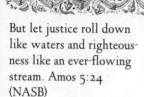

But let justice roll down like waters and righteousness like an ever-flowing stream. Amos 5:24 (NASB)

Laughter
(*see also* JOY)

And Sarah said, "God has made laughter for me; everyone who hears will laugh with me." Genesis 21:6 (NASB)

He will yet fill your mouth with laughter and your lips with shouts of joy. Job 8:21 (NIV)

A time to weep, and a time to laugh; a time to mourn, and a time to dance. Ecclesiastes 3:4 (KJV)

Then our mouth was filled with laughter, and our tongue with shouts of joy; then it was said among the nations, "The Lord has done great things for them." Psalms 126:2 (NRSV)

Blessed are you who hunger now, for you will be satisfied. Blessed are you who weep now, for you will laugh. Luke 6:21 (NIV)

Leadership
(*see also* POWER)

The human mind plans the way, but the Lord directs

the steps. Proverbs 16:9
(NRSV)

Where there is no vision,
the people are unrestrained.
Proverbs 29:18 (NASB)

And a little child shall lead
them. Isaiah 11:6 (NRSV)

Whoever wishes to be first
among you shall be slave of
all. Mark 10:44 (NASB)

Here is a trustworthy saying:
If anyone sets his heart on
being an overseer, he desires
a noble task. 1 Timothy 3:1
(NIV)

Learning

(*see also* EDUCATION *and*
WISDOM)

Instruct a wise man and he
will be wiser still; teach a
righteous man and he will
add to his learning. Proverbs
9:9 (NIV)

Wise people store up
knowledge, but the mouth of
a fool makes ruin imminent.
Proverbs 10:14 (NIV)

But go and learn what this
means: "I desire mercy, not
sacrifice." For I have not
come to call the righteous,
but sinners. Matthew 9:13
(NIV)

Take my yoke upon you, and
learn from me; for I am
gentle and humble in heart,

and you will find rest for your souls. Matthew 11:29 (NRSV)

Jesus increased in wisdom and stature, and in favor with God and man. Luke 2:52 (KJV)

At that very time He rejoiced greatly in the Holy Spirit, and said, "I praise Thee, O Father, Lord of heaven and earth, that Thou didst hide these things from the wise and intelligent and didst reveal them to babes. Yes, Father, for thus it was well-pleasing in Thy sight. Luke 10:21 (NASB)

You, however, continue in the things you have learned and become convinced of, knowing from whom you have learned them; and that from childhood you have known the sacred writings which are able to give you the wisdom that leads to salvation through faith which is in Christ Jesus. 1 Corinthians 10:14 (NASB)

Life
(*see also* AGING *and* DEATH)

And he said, "Naked I came from my mother's womb, And naked I shall return there. The Lord gave and the Lord has taken away. Blessed be the name of the Lord." Job 1:21 (NASB)

It is the Spirit who gives life; the flesh profits nothing; the words that I have spoken to you are spirit and are life. John 6:63 (NASB)

The thief comes only to steal, and kill, and destroy; I came that they might have life, and might have it abundantly. John 10:10 (NASB)

I am the resurrection and the life. Those who believe in me, even though they die will live, and everyone who lives and believes in me will never die. John 11:25–26 (NRSV)

Before long, the world will not see me anymore, but you will see me. Because I live, you also will live. John 14:19 (NIV)

No one has greater love than this, to lay down one's life for one's friends. John 15:13 (NRSV)

If we live, we live to the Lord; and if we die, we die to the Lord. So, whether we live or die, we belong to the Lord. Romans 14:8 (NIV)

Why, you do not even know what will happen tomorrow. What is your life? You

are a mist that appears for a little while and then vanishes. James 4:14 (NIV)

Blessed are those who wash their robes, that they may have the right to the tree of life, and may enter by the gates into the city. Revelation 22:14 (NASB)

Listening

(*see also* COMPASSION *and* WISDOM)

I will hear what God the Lord will say; for He will speak peace to His people, to His godly ones; but let them not turn back to folly. Psalms 85:8 (NASB)

Let the wise listen and add to their learning, and let the discerning get guidance. Proverbs 1:5 (NIV)

Incline your ear, and come to me; listen, so that you may live. Isaiah 55:3 (NRSV)

Then Jesus said, "He who has ears to hear, let him hear." Mark 4:9 (NIV)

My dear friends, you should be quick to listen, slow to speak or to get angry. James 1:19 (CEV)

Love

(*see also* DESIRE, HEART, *and* RELATIONSHIPS)

Hatred stirs up strife, but love covers all transgressions. Proverbs 10:12 (NASB)

Better is a dish of vegetables where love is, than a fattened ox and hatred with it. Proverbs 15:17 (NASB)

Let him kiss me with the kisses of his mouth—for your love is more delightful than wine. Song of Songs 1:2 (NIV)

His banner over me was love. Song of Songs 2:4 (KJV)

I am his, and he is mine, as he feeds his sheep among the lilies. Song of Songs 6:3 (CEV)

But I say to you, love your enemies, and pray for those who persecute you. Matthew 5:44 (NASB)

"The most important one," answered Jesus, "is this: 'Hear, O Israel, the Lord our God, the Lord is one. Love the Lord your God with all your heart and with all your soul and with all your mind and with all your strength.' The second is this: 'Love your neighbor as yourself.' There is no commandment greater than these." Mark 12:29–31 (NIV)

Love the Lord your God with all your heart and with all your soul and with all your mind and with all your strength. Mark 12:30 (NIV)

God so loved the world that he gave his only son, so that everyone who believes in him may not perish but may have eternal life. John 3:16 (NRSV)

A new command I give you: Love one another. As I have loved you, so you must love one another. John 13:34 (NIV)

Greater love has no one than this, that one lay down his life for his friends. John 15:13 (NASB)

Let love be without hypocrisy. Abhor what is evil; cling to what is good. Romans 12:9 (NASB)

Be devoted to one another in brotherly love. Honor one another above yourselves. Romans 12:10 (NIV)

Love is patient; love is kind; love is not envious or boastful or arrogant or rude. It does not insist on its own way; it is not irritable or resentful; it does not rejoice in wrongdoing, but rejoices in the truth. It bears all things, believes all things, hopes all things, endures all things. 1 Corinthians 13:4–7 (NRSV)

But now abide faith, hope, love, these three; but the greatest of these is love. 1 Corinthians 13:13 (NASB)

You, my brothers, were called to be free. But do not use your freedom to indulge the sinful nature; rather, serve one another in love. Galatians 5:13 (NIV)

And live a life of love, just as Christ loved us and gave himself up for us as a fragrant offering and sacrifice to God. Ephesians 5:2 (NIV)

Beloved, if God so loved us, we also ought to love one another. 1 John 4:11 (NASB)

There is no fear in love; but perfect love casts out fear, because fear involves punishment, and the one who fears is not perfected in love. 1 John 4:18 (NASB)

Marriage

(*see also* COMMITMENT, COMPANIONSHIP, LOVE, *and* RELATIONSHIPS)

For this cause a man shall leave his father and his mother, and shall cleave to his wife; and they shall become one flesh. Genesis 2:24 (NASB)

He who finds a wife finds what is good and receives favor from the Lord. Proverbs 18:22 (NIV)

Consequently they are no longer two, but one flesh. What therefore God has joined together, let no man separate. Matthew 19:6 (NASB)

But because of immoralities, let each man have his own wife, and let each woman have her own husband. Let the husband fulfill his duty to his wife, and likewise

also the wife to her husband. The wife does not have authority over her own body, but the husband does; and likewise also the husband does not have authority over his own body, but the wife does. 1 Corinthians 7:2-4 (NASB)

But if they cannot control themselves, they should marry, for it is better to marry than to burn with passion. 1 Corinthians 7:9 (NIV)

Be subject to one another out of reverence for Christ. Wives, be subject to your husbands as you are to the Lord. . . . Husbands, love your wives, just as Christ loved the church and himself up for her. . . . Husbands should love their wives as

they do their own bodies. He who loves his wife loves himself. Ephesians 6:21-22, 25, 28 (NRSV)

Husbands, love your wives, and do not be embittered against them. Colossians 3:19 (NASB)

Maturity
(*see also* ATTITUDE)

For we are but of yesterday, and know nothing, and because our days upon earth are a shadow. Job 8:9 (KJV)

For a thousand years in your sight are like a day that has just gone by, or like a watch in the night. Psalms 90:4 (NIV)

Do not let kindness and truth leave you; bind them around your neck, write them on the tablet of your heart. Proverbs 3:3 (NASB)

Better is a dish of vegetables where love is, than a fattened ox and hatred with it. Proverbs 15:17 (NASB)

When things are going well, enjoy yourself, and when they are going badly, consider this: God has designed the one no less than the other so that we should take nothing for granted. Ecclesiastes 7:14 (NJB)

Surely the nations are like a drop in a bucket; they are regarded as dust on the scales; he weighs the islands as though they were fine dust. Isaiah 40:15 (NIV)

And if your right eye offend thee, pluck it out, and cast it from thee: for it is profitable for thee that one of thine members should perish, and not that thy whole body would be cast into hell. Matthew 5:29 (KJV)

And human nature has nothing to look forward to but death, while the Spirit looks forward to life and peace. Romans 8:6 (NJB)

Mercy

(*see also* ACCEPTANCE, COMPASSION, FORGIVENESS, MISTAKES, *and* TOLERANCE)

This day you have seen with your own eyes how the Lord delivered you into my hands in the cave. Some urged me to kill you, but I spared you; I said, "I will not lift my hand against my master, because he is the Lord's anointed." 1 Samuel 24:10 (NIV)

Surely goodness and mercy shall follow me all the days of my life. Psalms 23:6 (KJV)

Mercy and truth are met together. Psalms 85:10 (KJV)

I will sing the mercies of the Lord forever. Psalms 89:1 (KJV)

The Lord our God is merciful and forgiving, even though we have rebelled against him. Daniel 9:9 (NIV)

Blessed are the merciful, for they shall obtain mercy. Matthew 5:7 (KJV)

But go and learn what this means: "I desire mercy, not sacrifice." For I have not come to call the righteous, but sinners. Matthew 9:13 (NIV)

Be merciful, just as your Father is merciful. Luke 6:36 (NIV)

"Which of these three do you think was a neighbor to

the man who fell into the hands of robbers?" The expert in the law replied, "The one who had mercy on him." Jesus told him, "Go and do likewise." Luke 10:36–37 (NIV)

It does not, therefore, depend on man's desire or effort, but on God's mercy. Romans 9:16 (NIV)

Messiah
(*see also* BELIEF *and* FAITHFULNESS)

Then it will come about in that day that the nations will resort to the root of Jesse, who will stand as a signal for the peoples; and His resting place will be glorious. Isaiah 11:10 (NASB)

Rejoice greatly, O Daughter of Zion! Shout, Daughter of Jerusalem! See, your king comes to you, righteous and having salvation, gentle and riding on a donkey, on a colt, the foal of a donkey. Zechariah 9:9 (NIV)

When he had called together all the people's chief priests and teachers of the law, he asked them where the

Christ was to be born. "In Bethlehem in Judea," they replied, "for this is what the prophet has written: 'But you, Bethlehem, in the land of Judah, are by no means least among the rulers of Judah; for out of you will come a ruler who will be the shepherd of my people Israel.'" Matthew 2:4–6 (NIV)

And Simon Peter answered and said, "Thou art the Christ, the Son of the living God." Matthew 16:16 (NASB)

The crowds that went ahead of him and those that followed shouted,

"Hosanna to the Son of David! Blessed is he who comes in the name of the Lord! Hosanna in the highest!" Matthew 21:9 (NIV)

False Christs and false prophets will arise, and will show signs and wonders, in order, if possible, to lead the elect astray. Mark 13:22 (NASB)

And He said to them, "O foolish men and slow of heart to believe in all that the prophets have spoken! "Was it not necessary for the Christ to suffer these things and to enter into His glory?" And beginning with Moses and

with all the prophets, He explained to them the things concerning Himself in all the Scriptures. Luke 24:25–27 (NASB)

The woman said, "I know that Messiah is coming. When he comes, he will explain everything to us." John 4:25 (NIV)

Everyone who believes that Jesus is the Christ is born of God, and everyone who loves the father loves his child as well. 1 John 5:1 (NIV)

Miracles
(see also HEALING)

Then Moses lifted up his hand and struck the rock twice with his rod; and water came forth abundantly, and the congregation and their beasts drank. Numbers 20:11 (NASB)

And behold, a leper came to Him, and bowed down to Him, saying, "Lord, if You are willing, You can make me clean." Matthew 8:2 (NASB)

But the centurion answered and said, "Lord, I am not worthy for You to come under my roof, but just say the word, and my servant will be healed." Matthew 8:8 (NASB)

Without warning, a furious storm came up on the lake, so that the waves swept over

the boat. But Jesus was sleeping. The disciples went and woke him, saying, "Lord, save us! We're going to drown!" He replied, "You of little faith, why are you so afraid?" Then he got up and rebuked the winds and the waves, and it was completely calm. The men were amazed and asked, "What kind of man is this? Even the winds and the waves obey him!" Matthew 8:24–27 (CEV)

"We have here only five loaves of bread and two fish," they answered. "Bring them here to me," he said. And he directed the people to sit down on the grass. Taking the five loaves and the two fish and looking up to heaven, he gave thanks and broke the loaves. Then

he gave them to the disciples, and the disciples gave them to the people. They all ate and were satisfied, and the disciples picked up twelve basketfuls of broken pieces that were left over. Matthew 14:17–20 (NIV)

Which is easier, to say to the paralytic, "Your sins are forgiven"; or to say, "Arise, and take up your pallet and walk?" Mark 2:9 (NASB)

And while the sun was setting, all who had any sick with various diseases brought them to Him; and laying His hands on every one of them, He was healing them. Luke 4:40 (NASB)

So he replied to the messengers, "Go back and report to

John what you have seen and heard: The blind receive sight, the lame walk, those who have leprosy are cured, the deaf hear, the dead are raised, and the good news is preached to the poor." Luke 7:22 (NIV)

When the people saw the sign that he had done, they began to say, "This is indeed the prophet who is come into the world." John 6:14 (NRSV)

He therefore answered, "Whether He is a sinner, I do not know; one thing I do know, that, whereas I was blind, now I see." John 9:25 (NASB)

And when He had said these things, He cried out with a loud voice, "Lazarus, come forth." He who had died came forth, bound hand and foot with wrappings; and his face was wrapped around with a cloth. Jesus said to them, "Unbind him, and let him go." John 11:43–44 (NASB)

God added his testimony by signs and wonders and various miracles, and by gifts of the Holy Spirit, distributed according to his will. Hebrews 2:4 (NRSV)

Mistakes

(*see also* BLAME, DISAPPOINT-MENT, HOPE, PATIENCE, PEACE, *and* RESPONSIBILITY)

Then Saul said, "I have sinned. Come back, David my son. Because you considered my life precious today, I will not try to harm you again. Surely I have acted like a fool and have erred greatly." 1 Samuel 26:21 (NIV)

You gave a wide place for my steps under me, and my feet did not slip. Psalms 18:26 (NRSV)

Do not let your hearts turn aside to her ways; do not stray into her paths. Proverbs 7:25 (NRSV)

Money
(see also VALUES and WEALTH)

A feast is made for laughter, and wine makes life merry, but money is the answer for everything. Ecclesiastes 10:19 (NIV)

No one can serve two masters; for either he will hate the one and love the other, or he will hold to one and despise the other. You cannot serve God and mammon. Matthew 6:24 (NASB)

For what does it profit a man to gain the whole world, and forfeit his soul? Mark 8:36 (NASB)

Then he said to them, "Watch out! Be on your guard against

all kinds of greed; a man's life does not consist in the abundance of his possessions." Luke 12:15 (NIV)

My God shall supply all your needs according to his riches in glory. Philippians 4:19 (GNB)

The love of money is the root of all evil. 1 Timothy 6:10 (KJV)

Morality

(*see also* GOD'S WILL, GOODNESS, *and* RIGHTEOUSNESS)

The Ten Commandments

1) Thou shalt have no other gods before me.

2) Thou shalt not make unto thee any graven image, . . . Thou shalt not bow down thyself to them, nor serve them: for I the Lord thy God am a jealous God, visiting the iniquity of the fathers upon the children unto the third and fourth generation of them that hate me; and shewing mercy unto thousands of them that love me, and keep my commandments.

3) Thou shalt not take the name of the Lord in vain; for the Lord will not hold him guiltless that taketh His name in vain.

4) Remember the Sabbath day, to keep it holy. Six days thou shalt labor, and do all thy work: But the seventh

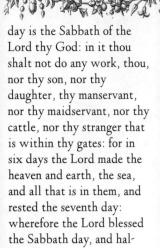

day is the Sabbath of the Lord thy God: in it thou shalt not do any work, thou, nor thy son, nor thy daughter, thy manservant, nor thy maidservant, nor thy cattle, nor thy stranger that is within thy gates: for in six days the Lord made the heaven and earth, the sea, and all that is in them, and rested the seventh day: wherefore the Lord blessed the Sabbath day, and hallowed it.

5) Honor thy father and mother: that thy days may be long upon the land which the Lord thy God giveth thee.

6) Thou shalt not kill.

7) Thou shalt not steal.

8) Thou shalt not commit adultery.

9) Thou shalt not bear false witness against thy neighbor.

10) Thou shalt not covet thy neighbor's house, thou shalt not covet thy neighbor's wife, nor his manservant, nor his maidservant, nor his ox, nor his ass, nor any thing that is his neighbor's.
Exodus 20:3–17 (KJV)

The righteous flourish like the palm tree, and grown like a cedar in Lebanon.
Psalms 92:12 (NRSV)

The righteous walk in integrity—happy are the children who follow them.
Proverbs 20:7 (NRSV)

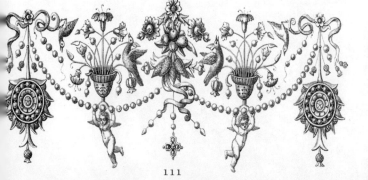

To do what is right and just is more acceptable to the Lord than sacrifice. Proverbs 21:3 (NIV)

Blessed are those who have been persecuted for the sake of righteousness, for theirs is the kingdom of heaven. Matthew 5:10 (NASB)

Flee the evil desires of youth, and pursue righteousness, faith, love and peace, along with those who call on the Lord out of a pure heart. 2 Timothy 2:22 (NIV)

To the pure, all things are pure; but to those who are defiled and unbelieving, nothing is pure, but both their mind and their conscience are defiled. Titus 1:15 (NASB)

Nature
(see also ENVIRONMENT)

He is the Maker of the Bear and Orion, the Pleiades and the constellations of the south. Job 9:9 (NIV)

Consider carefully the many wonders of God. Job 37:14 (CEV)

The Lord loves righteousness and justice; the earth is full of his unfailing love. Psalms 33:5 (NIV)

The meadows are covered with flocks and the valleys are mantled with grain; they shout for joy and sing. Psalms 65:13 (NIV)

The trees of the Lord are full of sap; the cedars of Lebanon,

which He planted; where the birds make their nests. Psalms 104:16–17 (KJV)

How many are your works, O Lord! In wisdom you made them all; the earth is full of your creatures. Psalms 104:24 (NIV)

For He spoke and raised up a stormy wind, which lifted up the waves of the sea. Psalms 107:25 (NASB)

There is an appointed time for everything. And there is a time for every event under heaven—A time to give birth, and a time to die; A time to plant, and a time to uproot what is planted. Ecclesiastes 3:1–2 (NASB)

Flowers are appearing on the earth. The season of glad songs has come, the cooing of the turtledove is heard in our land. Song of Songs 2:12 (NJB)

The desert and the parched land will be glad; the wilderness will rejoice and blossom. Like the crocus, it will burst into bloom; it will rejoice greatly and shout for joy. The glory of Lebanon will be given to it, the splendor of Carmel and Sharon; they will see the glory of the Lord, the splendor of our God. Isaiah 35:1–2 (NIV)

And why are you anxious about clothing? Observe how the lilies of the field grow; they do not toil nor do they spin, yet I say to you that even Solomon in all his glory did not clothe himself

like one of these. Matthew 6:28–29 (NASB)

The soil produces crops by itself; first the blade, then the head, then the mature grain in the head. Mark 4:28 (NASB)

Has not My hand made all these things? Acts 7:50 (NIV)

Need

(*see also* DESIRE *and* GENEROSITY)

For the poor will never cease to be in the land; therefore I command you, saying, "You shall freely open your hand to your brother, to your needy and poor in your land." Deuteronomy 15:11 (NASB)

Then he said to them, "Go, eat of the fat, drink of the sweet, and send portions to him who has nothing prepared; for this day is holy to our Lord. Nehemiah 8:10 (NASB)

They cause the cry of the poor to come unto him, and he heareth the cry of the afflicted. Job 34:28 (NIV)

The needy is not forgotten forever, not forever does the hope of the poor come to nothing. Psalms 9:18 (NJB)

The prayers of the homeless will be answered. Psalms 102:17 (CEV)

And my God shall supply all your needs according to His riches in glory in Christ Jesus. Philippians 4:19 (NASB)

Let us then approach the throne of grace with confidence, so that we may receive mercy and find grace to help us in our time of need. Hebrews 4:16 (NIV)

And the Spirit and the bride say, "Come." And let the one who hears say, "Come." And let the one who is thirsty come; let the one who wishes take the water of life without cost. Revelation 22:17 (NASB)

Neighbors

Thou shalt not bear false witness against thy neighbor. Thou shalt not covet thy neighbor's house, thou shalt not covet thy neighbor's wife, nor his manservant, nor his maidservant, nor his ox, nor his ass, nor any thing that is thy neighbor's. Exodus 20:16–17 (KJV)

You shall not take vengeance, nor bear any grudge against the sons of your people, but you shall love your neighbor as yourself; I am the Lord. Leviticus 19:18 (NASB)

Do not forsake your own friend or your father's friend, and do not go to your brother's house in the day of your calamity; better is a neighbor who is near than a brother far away. Proverbs 27:10 (NASB)

You shall love your neighbor as yourself. Mark 12:31 (NRSV)

Then Jesus asked, "Which one of these three people was a real neighbor to the man who was beaten up by robbers?" And the leader answered, "The one who showed pity." Jesus said to him, "Go and do the same." Luke 10:36-37 (CEV)

Love does no harm to its neighbor. Therefore love is the fulfillment of the law. Romans 13:10 (NIV)

Opportunity

(*see also* AMBITION, GOALS, *and* PERSEVERANCE)

Seek the Lord while he may be found; call on him while he is near. Isaiah 55:6 (NIV)

Ask, and it shall be given to you; seek, and ye shall find; knock, and it shall be opened to you: For every one that asketh receiveth, and he that seeketh findeth, and to him that knocketh it shall be opened. Matthew 7:7-8 (KJV)

So be on your guard! You don't know when your Lord will come.

Matthew 24:42 (CEV)

Do you not say, "Four months more and then the harvest"? I tell you, open your eyes and look at the fields! They are ripe for harvest. John 4:35 (NIV)

I am the door; if anyone enters through Me, he shall be saved, and shall go in and out, and find pasture. John 10:9 (NASB)

Jesus then said: "The light will be with you only a little longer now. Go on your way while you have the light, or darkness will overtake you, and

nobody who walks in the darkness knows where he is going." John 12:35 (NJB)

It is time to wake up. You know that the day when we will be saved is nearer now than when we first put our faith in the Lord. Romans 3:11 (CEV)

As we have therefore opportunity, let us do good unto all men. Galatians 6:10 (KJV)

Look, I am standing at the door, knocking. If one of you hears me calling and opens the door, I will come in to share a meal at that

person's side. Revelation 3:20 (NJB)

Parenting
(*see also* CHILDREN *and* FAMILY)

Honor your father and your mother, that your days may be prolonged in the land which the Lord your God gives you. Exodus 20:12 (NASB)

Only be careful, and watch yourselves closely so that you do not forget the things your eyes have seen or let them slip from your heart as long as you live. Teach them to your children and to their children after them. Deuteronomy 4:9 (NIV)

You shall teach them diligently to your sons and shall talk of them when you sit in your house and when you walk by the way and when you lie down and when you rise up. Deuteronomy 6:7 (NASB)

But from everlasting to everlasting the Lord's love is with those who fear him, and his righteousness with their children's children— with those who keep his covenant and remember to obey his precepts. Psalms 103:17–18 (NIV)

Teach your children right from wrong, and when they are grown they will still do right. Proverbs 22:6 (CEV)

Now I am ready to visit you for the third time, and I will not be a burden to you, because what I want is not your possessions but you. After all, children should not have to save up for their parents, but parents for their children. 2 Corinthians 12:14 (NIV)

Children, be obedient to your parents always, because that is what pleases the Lord. Colossians 3:20 (NJB)

Nothing brings me greater happiness than to hear that my children are obeying the truth. 3 John 1:4 (CEV)

Patience

(*see also* ACCEPTANCE, ANGER, DISAPPOINTMENT, FAITHFULNESS, *and* TESTS)

The hot-headed provoke disputes, the equable allay dissension. Proverbs 15:18 (NJB)

Better is the end of a thing than the beginning thereof, and patient in spirit is better than proud in spirit. Ecclesiastes 7:8 (KJV)

Do not be too easily exasperated, for exasperation dwells in the hearts of fools. Ecclesiastes 7:9 (NJB)

It is good that a man should both hope and wait for the salvation of the Lord. Lamentations 3:26 (KJV)

Now we exhort you, brethren, warn them that are unruly, comfort the feeble-minded, support the weak, be patient toward all men. 1 Thessalonians 5:14 (KJV)

Knowing this, the trying of your faith worketh patience. But let patience have her perfect work, that ye may be perfect and entire, wanting nothing. James 1:3–4 (KJV)

My dear brothers, take note of this: Everyone should be quick to listen, slow to speak and slow to become angry, for man's anger does not bring about the righteous life that God desires. James 1:19–20 (NIV)

Be patient, therefore, brethren, until the coming of the Lord. Behold, the farmer waits for the precious produce of the soil, being patient about it, until it gets the early and late rains. James 5:7 (NASB)

Peace
(*see also* CALM)

Then Moses departed and returned to Jethro his father-in-law, and said to him, "Please, let me go, that I may return to my brethren who are in Egypt, and see if they are still alive." And Jethro said to Moses, "Go in peace." Exodus 4:18 (NASB)

I will give peace in the land, and ye shall lie down, and none shall make you afraid: and I will rid evil beasts out of the land, neither shall the sword go through your land. Leviticus 26:6 (KJV)

Then Gideon built an altar there unto the Lord and named it The Lord is Peace. Judges 6:24 (KJV)

Depart from evil, and do good; seek peace, and pursue it. Psalms 34:14 (NASB)

Mercy and truth are met together; righteousness and peace have kissed each other. Psalms 85:10 (KJV)

I wait for the Lord, my soul waits, and in his word I hope; my soul waits for the Lord more than those who watch for the morning. Psalms 130:5–6 (NRSV)

How good and pleasant it is when brothers live together in unity! Psalms 133:1 (NIV)

When a man's ways are pleasing to the Lord, He makes even his enemies to be at peace with him. Proverbs 16:7 (NASB)

There is also a time for love and hate, for war and peace. Ecclesiastes 3:8 (CEV)

And He will judge between the nations, and will render decisions for many peoples; and they will hammer their swords into plowshares, and their spears into pruning hooks. Nation will not lift up sword against nation, and never again will they

learn war. Isaiah 2:4 (NASB)

The wolf also shall dwell with the lamb, and the leopard shall lie down with the kid; and the calf and the young lion and the fatling together; and a little child shall lead them. Isaiah 11:6 (KJV)

The fruit of righteousness will be peace; the effect of righteousness will be quietness and confidence forever. Isaiah 32:17 (NIV)

I will extend peace to her like a river. Isaiah 66:12 (KJV)

Every man will sit under his own vine and under his own fig tree, and no one will make them afraid, for the

Lord Almighty has spoken. Micah 4:4 (NIV)

Blessed are the peacemakers: they shall be recognized as children of God. Matthew 5:9 (NJB)

And the peace of God, which surpasses all comprehension, shall guard your hearts and your minds in Christ Jesus. Philippians 4:7 (NASB)

I have learned to be content with whatever I have. Philippians 4:11 (NRSV)

Peace I leave with you, my peace I give unto you. John 14:27 (KJV)

The fruit of the Spirit is love, joy, peace, patience, kindness, generosity, faith-

fulness, gentleness and self-control. Galatians 5:22 (NRSV)

For he is our peace; in his flesh he has made both groups into one and has broken down the dividing wall, that is, the hostility between us. Ephesians 2:14 (NRSV)

Let the peace of Christ rule in your hearts, to which indeed you were called in one body. Colossians 3:15 (NRSV)

The Lord direct your hearts unto the love of God, and into the patient waiting for Christ. 2 Thessalonians 3:5 (KJV)

Let us run with patience the race that is set before us. Hebrews 12:1 (KJV)

People of God

This is the written account of Adam's line. When God created man, he made him in the likeness of God. He created them male and female and blessed them. And when they were created, he called them "man." When Adam had lived 130 years, he had a son in his own likeness, in his own image; and he named him Seth. Genesis 5:1–3 (NIV)

And God said to Balaam, "Do not go with them; you shall not curse the people; for they are blessed." Numbers 22:12 (NASB)

Thy people shall be my people, and thy God my God. Ruth 1:16 (KJV)

The Lord is our God, and we are his people; the sheep he takes care of in his own pasture. Psalms 95:7 (CEV)

As for a human person—his days are like grass: he blows like the wildflowers, as soon as the wind blows he is gone, and never to be seen there again. Psalms 103:15–16 (KJV)

As the mountains surround Jerusalem, so the Lord surrounds His people from this time forth and forever. Psalms 125:2 (NASB)

"Comfort, O comfort My people," says your God. Isaiah 40:1 (KJV)

Yet, O Lord, you are our Father. We are the clay, you are the potter; we are all the work of your hand. Isaiah 64:8 (NASB)

And seeing the multitudes, He felt compassion for them, because they were distressed and downcast like sheep without a shepherd. Matthew 9:36 (NASB)

"This is the covenant I will make with the house of Israel after that time," declares the Lord. "I will put my laws in their minds and write them on their hearts. I will be their God, and they will be my people." Hebrews 8:10 (NIV)

But you are a chosen race, a royal priesthood, a holy nation, God's own people, in order that you may proclaim the mighty acts of him who called you out of darkness into his marvelous light. Once you were not a people, but now you are God's people; once you had not received mercy, but now you have received mercy. 1 Peter 2:9–10 (NRSV)

Perseverance

(*see also* ACTION, AMBITION, ENERGY, SUCCESS, *and* WORK ETHIC)

For they all made us afraid, saying, "Their hands shall be weakened from the work, that it be not done." Now, therefore, O God, strengthen my hands. Nehemiah 6:9 (KJV)

Anyone upright grows stronger step by step: and anyone whose hands are clean grows ever in rigor! Job 17:9 (NJB)

Do not swerve to the right or to the left;

turn your foot away from evil. Proverbs 4:27 (NRSV)

You grew weary from your many wanderings but you did not say, "It is useless." You found your desire rekindled and so you did not weaken. Isaiah 57:10 (NRSV)

Simon, Simon! Look, Satan has got his wish to sift you as wheat; but I have prayed for you, Simon, that your faith may not fail, and once you have recovered, you in your turn must strengthen your brothers! Luke 22:31–2 (NJB)

But the one who endures to the end will be saved. Mark 13:13 (NRSV)

And not only this, but we also exult in our tribulations, knowing that tribulation brings about perseverance; and perseverance, proven character; and proven character, hope. Romans 5:3–4 (NASB)

He will continue to give you strength till the very end, so that you will be irreproachable on the Day of our Lord Jesus Christ. 1 Corinthians 1:8 (NJB)

For we will reap at harvesttime, if we do not give up. Galatians 6:9 (NRSV)

Keep alert and always persevere in supplication for all the saints. Ephesians 6:18 (NRSV)

I have fought the good fight, I have finished my course, I have kept the faith. 2 Timothy 4:7 (KJV)

So do not throw away your confidence; it will be richly rewarded. You need to persevere so that when you have done the will of God, you will receive what he has promised. Hebrews 10:35–36 (NIV)

Blessed is the man who perseveres under trial, because when he has stood the test, he will receive the crown of life that God has promised to those who love him. James 1:12 (NIV)

Behold, we count those blessed who endured. You have heard of the endurance of Job and have seen the outcome of the Lord's dealings, that the Lord is full of compassion and is merciful. James 5:11 (NASB)

Anyone who proves victorious will inherit these things; and I will be his God and he will be my son. Revelation 21:7 (NJB)

Playfulness

David, wearing a linen ephod, danced before the Lord with all his might, while he and the entire house of Israel brought up the ark of the Lord with shouts and the sound of trumpets. 2 Samuel 6:14–15 (NIV)

Let the heavens be glad, and let the earth rejoice; let the sea roar, and all it contains. Psalms 96:11 (NASB)

And there are the ships, as well as the Leviathan, the monster you created to splash in the sea. Psalms 104:26 (CEV)

Let them praise His name in the dance; let them sing praises unto Him with the timbrel and harp. Psalms 149:3 (KJV)

Boys and girls will play in the streets. Zechariah 8:5 (CEV)

How fine, how splendid that will be, with what to make the young men flourish, and new wine the maidens! Zechariah 9:17 (NJB)

It is like children sitting in the marketplaces and calling to one another; we played the flute for you and you did not dance; we wailed and you did not mourn. Matthew 11:16 (NRSV)

Pleasure
(*see also* DESIRE *and* JOY)

And thou shalt rejoice in every good thing which the Lord thy God hath given unto thee and unto thine house. Deuteronomy 26:11 (KJV)

How very good and pleasant it is when kindred live together in unity! Psalms 133:1 (NRSV)

Stolen waters are sweet, and bread tastes better when eaten in secret. Proverbs 9:17 (NJB)

The poor have a hard life, but being content is as good as an endless feast. Proverbs 15:15 (CEV)

Folly appeals to someone without sense, a person of understanding goes straight forward. Proverbs 15:21 (NJB)

Moreover, that every man who eats and drinks sees good in all his labor—it is the gift of God. Ecclesiastes 3:13 (NASB)

So I commend the enjoyment of life, because nothing is better for a man under the sun than to eat and drink and be glad. Then joy will accompany him in his work all the days of the life God has given him under the sun. Ecclesiastes 8:15 (NIV)

Go then, eat your bread in happiness, and drink your wine with a cheerful heart; for God has already approved your works. Ecclesiastes 9:7 (NASB)

Power
(*see also* LEADERSHIP)

Know therefore today, and take it to your heart, that the Lord, He is God in heaven above and on the earth below; there is no other. Deuteronomy 4:39 (NASB)

Once God has spoken; Twice I have heard this: Strength belongs to God. Psalms 62:11 (NJB)

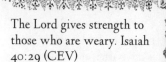

The Lord gives strength to those who are weary. Isaiah 40:29 (CEV)

And Jesus came to them and said: "I have been given all the authority in heaven and on earth!" Matthew 28:18 (CEV)

You will receive power when the Holy Spirit has come upon you. Acts 1:8 (NRSV)

Let every soul be subject to the higher powers. For there is no power but of God: the powers that be are ordained of God. Whosoever therefore resisteth the power resisteth the ordinance of God: and they that resist shall receive to themselves damnation. Romans 13:1–2 (KJV)

But to those whom God has called, both Jews and Greeks, Christ the power of God and the wisdom of God. 1 Corinthians 1:24 (NIV)

For the kingdom of God consists not in spoken words, but in power. 1 Corinthians 4:20 (NJB)

And He has said to me, "My grace is sufficient for you, for power is perfected in weakness." Most gladly, therefore, I will rather boast about my weaknesses, that the power of Christ may dwell in me. 2 Corinthians 12:9 (NASB)

I pray also that the eyes of your heart may be enlightened in order that you may know the hope to which he has called you, the riches of his glorious inheritance in the saints, and his incomparably great power for us who believe. That power is like the working of his mighty strength, which he exerted in Christ when he raised him from the dead and seated him at his right hand in the heavenly realms, far above all rule and authority, power and dominion, and every title that can be given, not only in the present age but also in the one to come. Ephesians 1:18–21 (NIV)

God did not give us a spirit of cowardice, but rather a spirit of power and love and self-reliance. 2 Timothy 1:7 (NRSV)

You have faith in God, whose power will protect you unto the last day. 1 Peter 1:5 (CEV)

Praising God

(*see also* GRATITUDE *and* WORSHIP)

Then sang Moses and the children of Israel this song unto the Lord, and spake, saying I will sing unto the Lord, for he hath triumphed gloriously: the horse and his rider hath he thrown into the sea. Exodus 15:1 (KJV)

The Lord lives! Praise be to my Rock! Exalted be God,

the Rock, my Savior!
2 Samuel 22:47 (NIV)

For great is the Lord,
and greatly to be
praised: he is to be
revered above all gods.
1 Chronicles 16:25
(NRSV)

Stand up and praise the
Lord your God, who is
from everlasting to
everlasting. "Blessed be
your glorious name, and
may it be exalted above
all blessing and praise."
Nehemiah 9:5 (NIV)

Many, O Lord my
God, are the wonders
which Thou hast done,
and Thy thoughts
toward us; there is
none to compare with

Thee; if I would
declare and speak of
them, they would be
too numerous to count.
Psalms 40:5 (NASB)

Be still, acknowledge
that I am God supreme
over nations, supreme
over the world. Psalms
46:10 (NJB)

So I always sing praises
to your name, as I pay
my vows day after day.
Psalms 61:8 (NRSV)

Let heaven and earth
praise Him, the seas
and everything that
moves in them. Psalms
69:34 (NASB)

O Come, let us sing
unto the Lord: let us
make a joyful noise to

the rock of our salvation. Psalms 95:1 (KJV)

Praise the Lord, O my soul; all my inmost being, praise His holy name. Praise the Lord, O my soul, and forget not all His benefits— who forgives all your sins and heals all your diseases, who redeems your life from the pit and crowns you with love and compassion, who satisfies your desires with good things so that your youth is renewed like the eagle's. Psalms 103:1–5 (NIV)

Oh that men would praise the Lord for his goodness, and for His wonderful works to the children of men! Psalms 107:8 (KJV)

Not to us, O Lord, not to us, but to Thy name give glory because of Thy lovingkindness, because of Thy truth. Psalms 115:1 (NASB)

O house of Levi, bless the Lord; You who revere the Lord, bless the Lord. Psalms 135:20 (NASB)

While I live will I praise the Lord: I will sing praises unto my God while I have any being. Psalms 146:2 (KJV)

Let everything that has breath praise the Lord.

Praise ye the Lord! Psalms 150:6 (KJV)

In that day you will say: Give thanks to the Lord, call on his name; make known among the nations what he has done, and proclaim that his name is exalted. Isaiah 12:4 (NIV)

O Lord, you are my God; I will exalt you and praise your name, for in perfect faithfulness you have done marvelous things, things planned long ago. Isaiah 25:1 (NIV)

The men said to Jesus, "Don't you hear what those children are saying?" "Yes I do!" Jesus answered. "Don't you know that the Scriptures say, 'Children and infants will sing praises'?" Matthew 21:16 (CEV)

And Mary said: "My soul exalts the Lord, and my spirit has rejoiced in God my Savior." Luke 1:46–47 (NASB)

God was very kind to us because of the Son he dearly loves, and so we should praise God. Ephesians 1:6 (CEV)

He even said to God, "I will tell them your name and sing your praises when they come together to worship." Hebrews 2:12 (CEV)

Through him, then, let us continually offer a sacrifice of praise to God, that is the fruit of lips that confess his name. Hebrews 13:15 (NRSV)

134

Then I heard what sounded like a great multitude, like the roar of rushing waters and like loud peals of thunder, shouting: "Hallelujah! For our Lord God Almighty reigns. Let us rejoice and be glad and give him glory! For the wedding of the Lamb has come, and his bride has made herself ready. Revelation 19:6–7 (NIV)

Prayer

(*see also* PRAISING GOD)

I prayed for this child, and the Lord has granted me what I asked of him. 1 Samuel 1:27 (NIV)

In my distress I called upon the Lord, and cried to my God: and he did hear my voice out of his temple, and my cry did enter his ears. 2 Samuel 22:7 (KJV)

May your eyes be open to the entreaty of your servant and to the entreaty of your people Israel, to listen to them, whatever they ask of you. 1 Kings 8:52 (NJB)

I cry out to Thee for help, but Thou dost not answer me; I stand up, and Thou dost turn Thy attention against me. Job 30:20 (NASB)

So that they cause the cry of the poor to come unto him, and he heareth the cry of the afflicted. Job 34:28 (KJV)

Blessed be the Lord, because He has heard the voice of my supplication. Psalms 28:6 (NASB)

Pray to Me in time of trouble. I will rescue you, and you will honor me. Psalms 50:15 (CEV)

From a sea of troubles I call out to you, O Lord. Psalms 130:1 (CEV)

The sacrifice of the wicked is an abomination to the Lord, but the prayer of the upright is His delight. Proverbs 15:8 (NASB)

Also, seek the peace and prosperity of the city to which I have carried you into exile. Pray to the Lord for it, because if it prospers, you too will prosper. Jeremiah 29:7 (NIV)

Listen, my God, listen to us; open your eyes and look at our plight and at the city that bears your name. Relying not on our upright deeds but on your great mercy we pour out our plea to you. Daniel 9:18 (NJB)

In my distress I called to the Lord, and he answered me. From the depths of the grave I called for help, and you listened to my cry. Jonah 2:2 (NIV)

Whenever you pray, go into your room and shut the door and pray to your Father who is in secret; and your Father who sees in secret will reward you. And when you

are praying, do not use meaningless repetition, as the Gentiles do, for they suppose that they will be heard for their many words. Therefore do not be like them; for your Father knows what you need, before you ask Him. Matthew 6:6–8 (NRSV)

The Lord's Prayer

Our Father which art in heaven, Hallowed be Thy name. Thy kingdom come. Thy will be done, in earth, as it is in heaven. Give us this day our daily bread. And forgive us our debts, as we also forgive our debtors. And lead us not into temptation, but deliver us from evil: For Thine is the kingdom, and the power, and the glory, forever.

Amen. Matthew 6:9–13 (KJV)

Ask, and you will receive. Search, and you will find. Knock and the door will be opened to you. Everyone who asks will receive. Everyone who searches will find. And the door will be opened for everyone who knocks. Matthew 7:7–8

And all things you ask in prayer, believing, you shall receive. Matthew 21:22 (NASB)

Everything you ask for in prayer will be yours, if you only have faith. And when you stand in prayer, forgive whatever you have against anybody, so that your Father in heaven may forgive your

failings, too. Mark
11:24–25 (NJB)

Pray without ceasing.
1 Thessalonians 5:17 (KJV)

I will therefore that men
pray every where, lifting up
holy hands, without wrath
and doubting. 1 Timothy 2:8
(KJV)

The prayer offered in faith
will restore the one who is
sick, and the Lord will raise
him up, and if he has com-
mitted sins, they will be forgiven him. Therefore, confess
your sins to one another, and
pray for one another, so that
you may be healed. The effective prayer of a righteous
man can accomplish much.
James 5:15–16 (NASB)

The Present
(*see also* THE FUTURE, TIME,
and TOMORROW)

Do not congratulate yourself
about tomorrow, since you
do not know what today
will bring forth. Proverbs
27:1 (NJB)

Do not say, "Why were the
old days better than these?"
For it is not wise to ask such
questions. Ecclesiastes 7:10
(NIV)

He did it to demonstrate his
justice at the present time,
so as to be just and the one
who justifies those who
have faith in Jesus. Romans
3:26 (NASB)

For I reckon that the sufferings of the present time are

not worthy to be compared with the glory which shall be revealed in us. Romans 8:18 (KJV)

What I mean, brothers, is that the time is short. From now on those who have wives should live as if they had none; those who mourn, as if they did not; those who are happy, as if they were not; those who buy something, as if it were not theirs to keep; those who use the things of the world, as if not engrossed in them. For this world in its present form is passing away. 1 Corinthians 7:29–31 (NIV)

Now is the acceptable time; now is the day of salvation. 2 Corinthians 6:2 (KJV)

Make the best of the present time, for it is a wicked age. Ephesians 5:16 (NJB)

By the same word the present heavens and earth are reserved for fire, being kept for the day of judgment and destruction of ungodly men. 2 Peter 3:7 (NIV)

Priorities
(*see also* RESPONSIBILITY)

Teach us to count up the days that are ours, and we shall come to the heart of wisdom. Psalms 90:12 (NJB)

Do not wear yourself out to get rich; have the wisdom to

show restraint. Proverbs 23:4 (NIV)

But lay up for yourselves treasures in heaven, where neither moth nor rust doth corrupt, and where thieves do not break through or steal. Matthew 6:20 (KJV)

But seek first His kingdom and His righteousness; and all these things shall be added to you. Matthew 6:33 (NASB)

He who loves father or mother more than Me is not worthy of Me; and he who loves son or daughter more than Me is not worthy of Me. Matthew 10:37 (NASB)

Now he who plants and he who waters are one; but

each will receive his own reward according to his own labor. 1 Corinthians 3:8 (NASB)

Know ye not that they which run in a race run all, but one receiveth the prize? So run, that ye may obtain the prize. 1 Corinthians 9:24 (KJV)

But earnestly desire the greater gifts. And I show you a still more excellent way. If I speak with the tongues of men and of angels, but do not have love, I have become a noisy gong or a clanging cymbal. 1 Corinthians 12:31–13:1 (NASB)

So, my dear brothers, keep firm and immovable, always abounding in energy for the

Lord's work, being sure that in the Lord none of your labors is wasted. 1 Corinthians 15:58 (NJB)

While we look not at the things which are seen, but at the things which are not seen; for the things which are seen are temporal, but the things which are not seen are eternal. 2 Corinthians 4:18 (KJV)

More than that, I count all things to be loss in view of the surpassing value of knowing Christ Jesus my Lord, for whom I have suffered the loss of all things, and count them but rubbish in order that I may gain Christ. Philippians 3:8 (NASB)

I press on toward the goal to win the prize for which God has called me heavenward in Christ Jesus. Philippians 3:14 (NIV)

You have been raised to life with Christ. Now the forces of the universe don't have any power over you. Colossians 3:1 (CEV)

And over all these virtues put on love, which binds them all together in perfect unity. Colossians 3:14 (NIV)

Prove all things; hold fast to that which is good. 1 Thessalonians 5:21 (KJV)

But as someone dedicated to God, avoid all that. You must aim to be upright and religious, filled with faith and love, perseverance and

gentleness. 1 Timothy 6:11 (NJB)

Productivity

(*see also* ACTION, ENERGY, FULFILLMENT, *and* SUCCESS)

Ye shall not do after all the things we do here this day, every man whatsoever is right in his own eyes. Deuteronomy 12:8 (KJV)

They became hewers of wood and drawers of water for the whole congregation, just as the leaders had spoken to them. Joshua 9:21 (NASB)

Ants are creatures of little strength, yet they store up their food in the summer. Proverbs 30:25 (NIV)

Whatsoever thy hand findeth to do, do it with thy might; for there is no work, nor device, nor knowledge, nor wisdom, in the grave, whither thou goest. Ecclesiastes 9:10 (KJV)

By your great skill in trading you have increased your wealth, and because of your wealth your heart has grown proud. Ezekiel 28:5 (NIV)

So, dear brothers, keep firm and immovable, always abounding in energy for the Lord's work, being sure that in the Lord none of your labors is wasted. 1 Corinthians 15:58 (KJV)

Remember this: Whoever sows sparingly will also reap sparingly, and whoever sows generously will also reap generously. 2 Corinthians 9:6 (NIV)

Don't delude yourself: God is not to be fooled; whatever someone sows, that is what he will reap. Galatians 6:7 (NJB)

As scripture says: "You must not muzzle an ox when it is treading out the corn," and again: "The worker deserves his wages." 1 Timothy 5:18 (NJB)

Protection

(*see also* ANXIETY, FEAR, *and* SECURITY)

Of Benjamin he said, "The beloved of the Lord shall dwell in safety by him; and the Lord shall cover him all the day long, and he shall dwell between his shoulders." Deuteronomy 33:12 (KJV)

My God, my rock, in whom I take refuge; my shield and the horn of my salvation, my stronghold and my refuge; my savior, Thou dost save me from violence. 2 Samuel 22:3 (NASB)

Thou hast enlarged my steps under me so that my feet did not slip. 2 Samuel 22:37 (KJV)

Rather, worship the Lord your God; it is he who will deliver you from the hand of all your enemies. 2 Kings 17:39 (NIV)

The Lord is a refuge for the oppressed, a stronghold in times of trouble. Psalms 9:9 (NIV)

Keep me as the apple of the eye; hide me in the shadow of Thy wings, from the wicked who despoil me, my deadly enemies, who surround me. Psalms 17:8–9 (NASB)

The Lord is my rock and my fortress and my deliverer, My God, my rock, in whom I take refuge; my shield and the horn of my salvation, my stronghold. Psalms 18:2 (NASB)

Yea, though I walk through the valley of the shadow of death, I will fear no evil: for thou art with me; thy rod and thy staff, they comfort me. Psalms 23:4 (KJV)

Be merciful to me, O God, be merciful unto me: for my soul trusteth in thee: Yea, in the shadow of thy wings will I make my refuge, until these calamities be overpast. Psalms 57:1 (KJV)

For he will command his angels concerning you to guard you in all your ways. Psalms 91:11 (NRSV)

The sun will not smite you by day, nor the moon by night. The Lord will protect you from all evil; He will keep your soul. Psalms 121:6-7 (NASB)

He is a shield to those who take refuge in him. Proverbs 30:5 (NRSV)

They will live there in safety and will build houses and plant vineyards; they will live in safety when I inflict punishment on all their neighbors who

maligned them. Then they will know that I am the Lord their God. Ezekiel 28:26 (NIV)

My God hath sent his angel, and hath shut the lions' mouths, that they have not hurt me. Daniel 6:22 (KJV)

Seek the Lord, all you humble of the earth who have carried out His ordinances; seek righteousness, seek humility. Perhaps you will be hidden in the day of the Lord's anger. Zephaniah 2:3 (NASB)

The Spirit of the Lord is on me, because he has anointed me to

preach good news to the poor. He has sent me to proclaim freedom for the prisoners and recovery of sight for the blind, to release the oppressed, to proclaim the year of the Lord's favor. Luke 4:18–19 (NIV)

I am with you. I have so many people that belong to me in this city that no one will attempt to hurt you. Acts 18:10 (NJB)

But in all these things we overwhelmingly conquer through Him who loved us. Romans 8:37 (NASB)

Recovery

(*see also* FAITHFULNESS, HEALING, *and* REDEMPTION)

When you are in distress and all these things have come upon you, in the latter days, you will return to the Lord your God and listen to His voice. For the Lord your God is a compassionate God; He will not fail you nor destroy you nor forget the covenant with your fathers which He swore to them. Deuteronomy 4:30–31 (NASB)

For he who wounds is he who soothes the sore, and the hand that hurts is the hand that heals. Job 5:18 (NJB)

"Let us break their chains," they say, "and throw off

their fetters." Psalms 2:3 (NIV)

A joyful heart is good medicine, but a broken spirit dries up the bones. Proverbs 17:22 (NASB)

A time to kill, and a time to heal; a time to break down, and a time to build up. Ecclesiastes 3:3 (KJV)

The Lord God will wipe away tears from off all faces. Isaiah 25:8 (KJV)

But he was pierced for our transgressions, he was crushed for our iniquities; the punishment that brought us peace was upon him, and by his wounds we are healed. Isaiah 53:5 (NIV)

Heal me, O Lord, and I will be healed; save me and I will be saved, for Thou art my praise. Jeremiah 17:14 (NASB)

They shall ask the way to Zion with their faces thitherward, saying, Come, and let us join ourselves to the Lord in a perpetual covenant that shall not be forgotten. Jeremiah 50:5 (KJV)

I, the Lord, have rebuilt the ruined places, and replanted that which was desolate. Ezekiel 36:36 (NRSV)

Thus says the Lord to these bones: I will cause breath to enter you, and you shall live. Ezekiel 37:5 (NRSV)

Restore us to yourself, O Lord, that we may return;

renew our days as of old.
Lamentations 5:21 (NIV)

Come, and let us return unto
the Lord: for he hath torn,
and he will heal us; he hath
smitten, and he will bind us
up. Hosea 6:1 (KJV)

The centurion answered,
"Lord, I am not worthy to
have you come under my roof;
but only speak the word, and
my servant will be healed."
Matthew 8:8 (NRSV)

Jesus answered them, "Go
and tell John what you hear
and see: the blind receive
their sight, the lame walk,
the lepers are cleansed, the
deaf hear, and the dead are
raised, and the poor have
good news brought to them."
Matthew 11:4–5 (NRSV)

If your brother sins against
you, go and show him his
fault, just between the two
of you. If he listens to you,
you have won your brother
over. Matthew 18:15 (NIV)

Simon, Simon, Satan has
asked to sift you as wheat.
But I have prayed for you,
Simon, that your faith may
not fail. And when you have
turned back, strengthen your
brothers. Luke 22:31–32
(NIV)

Remember this: Whoever
turns a sinner from the error
of his way will save him
from death and cover over a
multitude of sins. James 5:20
(NIV)

For you were continually
straying like sheep, but now

you have returned to the shepherd and guardian of your souls. 1 Peter 2:25 (NASB)

Then the One sitting on the throne spoke. "Look, I am making the whole of creation new. Write this, what I am saying is trustworthy and will come true." Revelation 21:5 (KJV)

Redemption
(*see also* MERCY)

God will redeem my soul from the power of the grave. Psalms 49:15 (KJV)

He sent redemption unto his people: he hath commanded his covenant for ever: holy

and reverend is his name. Psalms 111:9 (KJV)

But now, thus says the Lord, your Creator, O Jacob, and He who formed you, O Israel, do not fear, for I have redeemed you; I have called you by name; you are Mine! Isaiah 43:1 (NASB)

The ransomed of the Lord will return. They will enter Zion with singing; everlasting joy will crown their heads. Gladness and joy will overtake them, and sorrow and sighing will flee away. Isaiah 51:11 (NIV)

In his love and in his pity he redeemed them. Isaiah 63:9 (NRSV)

The next day he saw Jesus coming to him, and said,

"Behold, the Lamb of God who takes away the sin of the world!" John 1:29 (NASB)

For God so loved the world that he gave his only Son so that everyone who believes in him may not perish but may have eternal life. Indeed God did not send the Son into the world to condemn the world, but in order that the world might be saved through him. John 3:16–17 (NRSV)

God paid a great price for you. So do not become slaves of anyone else. 1 Corinthians 7:23 (CEV)

Christ redeemed us from the curse of the law by becoming a curse for us, for it is written: "Cursed is everyone who is hung on a tree." Galatians 3:13 (NIV)

In whom we have redemption through his blood, the forgiveness of our sins, according to the riches of his grace, wherein he hath abounded toward us in all wisdom and prudence. Ephesians 1:7–8 (KJV)

For He delivered us from the domain of darkness, and transferred us to the kingdom of His beloved Son, in whom we have redemption, the forgiveness of sins. Colossians 1:13–14 (NASB)

Neither by the blood of goats and calves, but by his own blood he entered in once into the holy place,

having obtained eternal redemption for us. Hebrews 9:12 (KJV)

But if we walk in the light, as he is in the light, we have fellowship with one another, and the blood of Jesus, his Son, purifies us from all sin. 1 John 1:7 (NIV)

Rejection

(*see also* DISAPPOINTMENT *and* TROUBLED TIMES)

For the Lord will not forsake his people for his great name's sake: because it hath pleased the Lord to make you his people. 1 Samuel 12:22 (KJV)

And Samuel said unto Saul, I will not return with thee: for thou hast rejected the word of the Lord, and the Lord hath rejected thee from being king over Israel. 1 Samuel 15:26 (KJV)

May the Lord our God be with us as he was with our fathers; may he never leave us nor forsake us. 1 Kings 8:57 (NIV)

As for you, my son Solomon, know the God of your father, and serve Him with a whole heart and a willing mind; for the Lord searches all hearts, and understands every intent of the thoughts. If you seek Him, He will let you find Him; but if you forsake Him, He will reject you forever. 1 Chronicles 28:9 (NASB)

The stone that the builders rejected has become the chief cornerstone. Psalms 118:22 (NRSV)

Believe me, God neither spurns anyone of integrity, nor lends his aid to the evil. Job 8:20 (NJB)

While you were doing all these things, declares the Lord, I spoke to you again and again, but you did not listen; I called you, but you did not answer. Jeremiah 7:13 (NIV)

"The one who listens to you listens to Me, and the one who rejects you rejects Me; and he who rejects Me rejects the One who sent Me." Luke 10:16 (NASB)

He came to His own, and those who were His own did not receive Him. John 1:11 (NASB)

I will not leave you comfortless: I will come to you. John 14:18 (KJV)

What I am saying is this: is it possible that God abandoned his own people? Out of the question! Romans 11:1 (NJB)

Put avarice out of your lives and be content with what you have; God himself has said: I

shall not fail you or desert you. Hebrews 13:5 (NJB)

Relationships
(*see also* COMPANION-SHIP, FRIENDSHIP, LOVE, *and* MARRIAGE)

So Jacob served seven years for Rachel and they seemed to him but a few days because of his love for her. Genesis 29:20 (NASB)

Thou shalt not avenge, nor bear any grudge against the children of thy people, but thou shalt love thy neighbor as thyself: I am the Lord. Leviticus 19:18 (KJV)

And she said unto him, How canst thou say, "I love thee," when thine heart is not with me? Thou hast mocked me these three times, and hast not told me wherein thy great strength lieth. Judges 16:15 (KJV)

How blessed is anyone who rejects the advice of the wicked and does not take a stand in the path that sinners tread, nor a seat in company with cynics. Psalms 1:1 (NJB)

Whoever walks with the wise becomes wise,

whoever mixes with fools will be ruined. Proverbs 13:20 (NJB)

An intelligent child is one who keeps the Law; an associate of profligates brings shame on his father. Proverbs 28:7 (NJB)

Have we not all one Father? Did not one God create us? Why do we profane the covenant of our fathers by breaking faith with one another? Malachi 2:10 (NIV)

Do not be deceived: "Bad company corrupts good morals." 1 Corinthians 15:33 (NASB)

We should help people whenever we can, especially if they are followers of the Lord. Galatians 6:10 (CEV)

Beloved, if God so loved us, we also ought to love one another. 1 John 4:11 (NASB)

And he has given us this command: Whoever loves God must also love his brother. 1 John 4:21 (NIV)

Responsibility
(*see also* DUTY *and* JUSTICE)

Am I my brother's keeper? Genesis 4:9 (KJV)

He asked the Lord, "Why have you brought this trouble on your servant? What have I done to displease you that you put the burden of all these people on me?" Numbers 11:11 (NIV)

Every man shall be put to death for his own sin. Deuteronomy 24:16 (KJV)

When David saw the angel who was striking down the people, he said to the Lord, "I am the one who has sinned and done wrong. These are but sheep. What have they done? Let your hand fall upon me and my family." 2 Samuel 24:17 (NIV)

Yet he did not put their sons to death, but acted in accordance with what is written in the Law, in the Book of Moses, where the Lord commanded: "Fathers shall not be put to death for their children, nor children put to death for their fathers; each is to die for his own sins." 2 Chronicles 25:4 (NIV)

But each will die for his own guilt. Everyone who eats unripe grapes will have his own teeth set on edge. Jeremiah 31:30 (NJB)

But I tell you that men will have to give account on the day of judgment for every careless word they have spoken. Matthew 12:36 (NIV)

But the one who does not know and does things deserving punishment will be beaten with few blows. From everyone who has been given much, much will be demanded; and from the one who has been entrusted with much, much more will be asked. Luke 12:48 (NIV)

Then said Jesus, Father, forgive them: for they know not what they do. Luke 23:34a (KJV)

We then that are strong ought to bear the infirmities of the weak, and not to please ourselves. Romans 15:1 (KJV)

Carry each other's burdens; that is how to keep the law of Christ. Galatians 6:2 (NJB)

For each one shall bear his own load. Galatians 6:5 (NASB)

But if anyone does not provide for his own, and especially for those of his household, he has denied the faith, and is worse than an unbeliever. 1 Timothy 5:8 (NASB)

Obey your leaders and do what they say. They are watching over you, and they must answer to God. So don't make them sad as they do their work. Make them happy. Otherwise, they won't be able to help you at all. Hebrews 13:17 (CEV)

If God so loved us, we ought also to love one another. 1 John 4:11 (KJV)

Restraint
(*see also* PATIENCE)

How shall I curse someone whom God has not cursed, denounce someone God has

not denounced? Numbers 23:8 (NJB)

May the Lord judge between you and me. And may the Lord avenge the wrongs you have done to me, but my hand will not touch you. 1 Samuel 24:12 (NIV)

Thus saith the Lord, "Ye shall not go up, nor fight against your brethren: return every man to his house: for this thing is done of Me. And they obeyed the words of the Lord, and returned from going against Jeroboam." 2 Chronicles 11:4 (NJB)

Do not be like a horse or a mule, without understanding, whose temper must be crushed with bit and bridle. Psalms 32:9 (NRSV)

Set a guard over my mouth, O Lord, keep watch over the door of my lips. Psalms 141:3 (NRSV)

When words are many transgressions are not lacking, but the prudent are restrained in speech. Proverbs 10:19 (NRSV)

Whoever looks down on a neighbor lacks good sense; the intelligent keeps a check on the tongue. Proverbs 11:12 (NJB)

The hot-headed provoke disputes, the equable allay dissension. Proverbs 15:18 (NJB)

Watch kept over mouth and tongue keeps the watcher

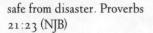

safe from disaster. Proverbs 21:23 (NJB)

But I tell you, Do not resist an evil person. If someone strikes you on the right cheek, turn to him the other also. Matthew 5:39 (NIV)

One of Jesus' followers pulled out a sword. He struck the servant of the high priest and cut off his ear. But Jesus told him, "Put your sword away. Anyone who lives by fighting will die by fighting." Matthew 26:51–52 (CEV)

Do not upright to excess and do not make yourself unduly wise: why should you destroy yourself? Ecclesiastes 7:16 (NJB)

If you think you are being religious, but you can't control your tongue, you are fooling yourself, and everything you do is useless. James 1:26 (CEV)

Rewards
(*see also* BLESSINGS, SUCCESS, VICTORY, *and* WEALTH)

After this, the word of the Lord came to Abram in a vision: Do not be afraid, Abram. I am your shield, your very great reward. Genesis 15:1 (NIV)

The Lord supports the afflicted; He brings down the wicked to the ground. Psalms 147:6 (NASB)

He who troubles his own house will inherit wind, and the foolish will be servant to the wisehearted. Proverbs 11:29 (NASB)

Rejoice, and be exceeding glad, for great is your reward in heaven: for so persecuted they the prophets which were before you. Matthew 5:12 (KJV)

For if you love those who love you, what reward do you have? Do not even the tax collectors do the same? Matthew 5:46 (NRSV)

Your Father knows what is done in secret, and he will reward you. Matthew 6:4 (CEV)

Anyone who welcomes a prophet just because that person is a prophet, will be given the same reward as a prophet. Anyone who welcomes a good person, just because that person is a good person, will be given the same reward as a good person. Matthew 10:41–42 (CEV)

For the Son of man is going to come in the glory of the Father with his angels, and then he will reward each one according to his behavior. Matthew 16:27 (KJV)

Long ago your own people did these same things to the prophets. So when this happens to you, be happy and jump for joy! You will have a great reward in heaven. Luke 6:23 (CEV)

But love your enemies and be good to them. Lend without expecting to be paid back. Then you will get a great reward, and you will be the true children of God in heaven. Luke 6:35 (CEV)

"And we indeed justly, for we are receiving what we deserve for our deeds; but this man has done nothing wrong." Luke 23:41 (NASB)

I press on towards the goal for the prize of the heavenly call of God in Christ Jesus. Philippians 3:14 (NRSV)

Righteousness
(*see also* GOODNESS *and* VIRTUE)

Divine

For the Lord is righteous; he loves righteousness; the upright will behold His face. Psalms 11:7 (NASB)

Glorious and majestic are his deeds, and his righteousness endures forever. Psalms 111:3 (NIV)

The good news tells how God accepts everyone who has faith, whether they are Jews or Gentiles. Romans 1:17 (CEV)

David says the same thing when he speaks of the blessedness of the man to whom God credits righteousness apart from works. Romans 4:6 (NIV)

For the fruit of the Spirit is in all goodness and righteousness and truth; proving what is acceptable unto the Lord. Ephesians 5:9–10 (KJV)

But about the Son he says, "Your throne, O God, will last for ever and ever, and righteousness will be the scepter of your kingdom." Hebrews 1:8 (NIV)

Human

Ye shall do no unrighteousness in judgment; thou shalt not respect the person of the poor, nor honor the person of the mighty: but in righteousness shalt thou judge thy neighbor. Leviticus 19:15 (KJV)

In the land of Uz there lived a man whose name was Job. This man was blameless and upright; he feared God and shunned evil. Job 1:1 (NIV)

He guides me in paths of saving justice as befits his name. Psalms 23:3 (NJB)

Now I am old, but ever since my youth I never saw an upright person abandoned, or the descendants of the upright forced to beg their bread. Psalms 37:25 (NJB)

The righteous shall flourish like the palm tree: he shall grow like a cedar in Lebanon. Psalms 92:12 (KJV)

To do what is right and just is more acceptable to the Lord than sacrifice. Proverbs 21:3 (NIV)

Blessed are those who hunger and thirst for righteousness, for they will be filled. Matthew 5:6 (NIV)

Blessed are those who have been persecuted for the sake of righteousness, for theirs is the kingdom of heaven. Matthew 5:10 (NASB)

There is no one righteous, not even one; there is no one who understands, no one who seeks God. Romans 3:10–11 (NIV)

My brothers, never slacken in doing what is right. 2 Thessalonians 3:13 (NJB)

From now on there is reserved for me the crown of righteousness. 2 Timothy 4:8 (NRSV)

Evil people will keep on being evil, and everyone who is dirty-minded will still be dirty-minded. But good people will keep on doing right, and God's people will always be holy. Revelation 22:11 (CEV)

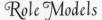

Role Models

Do not follow the crowd in doing wrong. When you give testimony in a lawsuit, do not pervert justice by siding with the crowd. Exodus 23:2 (NIV)

How blessed is anyone who rejects the advice of the wicked and does not take a stand in the path that sinners tread, nor take a seat in company with cynics. Psalms 1:1 (NJB)

Do not envy a man of violence, and do not choose any of his ways. Proverbs 3:31 (NASB)

For I have given you an example, that ye should do as I do unto you. John 13:15 (KJV)

And be not conformed to this world: but be ye transformed by the renewing of your mind, that ye may prove what is that good, and acceptable, and perfect will of God. Romans 12:2 (KJV)

You know how you should take us as your model: we were not undisciplined when we were with you, nor did we ever accept food from anyone without paying for it; no, we worked with unsparing energy, night and day, so as not to be a burden to any of you. This was not because we had no right to be, but in order to make ourselves a model for you to imitate. 2 Thessalonians 3:7–9 (NJB)

Don't let anyone make fun of you, just because you are

163

young. Set an example to other followers by what you say and do, as well as by your love, faith, and purity. 1 Timothy 4:12 (CEV)

We do not want you to become lazy, but to imitate those who through faith and patience inherit what has been promised. Hebrews 6:12 (NIV)

Such a large crowd of witnesses is all around us! So we must get rid of everything that slows us down, especially the sin that just won't let go. And we must be determined to run the race that is ahead of us. We must keep our eyes on Jesus, who leads us and makes our faith complete. He endured the shame of being nailed to a cross, because he knew that later on he would be glad he did. Now he is seated at the right side of God's throne! So keep your mind on Jesus, who puts up with many insults from sinners. Then you won't get discouraged and give up. Hebrews 12:1–3 (CEV)

Remember those who led you, who spoke the word of God to you; and considering the result of their conduct, imitate their faith. Hebrews 13:7 (NASB)

But as he which hath called you is holy, so be ye holy in all manner of conversation; because it is written, Be ye holy, for I am holy. 1 Peter 1:15–16 (KJV)

Security

I will both lie down and sleep in peace; for you alone, O Lord, make me lie down in safety. Psalms 4:8 (NRSV)

From the ends of the earth I call to you, I call as my heart grows faint; lead me to the rock that is higher than I. Psalms 61:2 (NIV)

Then you will walk on your way securely and your foot will not stumble. Proverbs 3:23 (NRSV)

To be afraid of human beings is a snare, whoever trusts in the Lord is secure. Proverbs 29:25 (NJB)

Anyone who hears and obeys these teachings of mine is like a wise person who built a house on solid rock. Rain poured down, rivers flooded, and winds beat against that house. But it did not fall, because it was built on solid rock. Matthew 7:24–25 (CEV)

When Jesus spoke again to the people, he said, "I am the light of the world. Whoever follows me will never walk in darkness, but will have the light of life." John 8:12 (NIV)

The sheep that belong to me listen to my voice; I know them and they follow me. I give them eternal life; they will never be lost and no one will ever steal them from my hand. John 10:27–28 (NJB)

What shall we then say to these things? If God be for

us, who can be against us? Romans 8:31 (KJV)

For I am convinced that neither death nor life nor anything else in all creation will be able to separate us from the love of God in Christ Jesus our Lord. Romans 8:38–39 (NRSV)

So we can say with confidence, "The Lord is my helper; I will not be afraid. What can anyone do to me?" Hebrews 13:6 (NRSV)

Self-esteem
(*see also* CHARACTER)

Then shalt thou prosper, if thou takest heed to fulfill the statutes and the judgments which the Lord charged Moses with concerning Israel: be strong, and of good courage, dread not, nor be dismayed. 1 Chronicles 22:13 (KJV)

Let Him weigh me with accurate scales, and let God know my integrity. Job 31:6 (NASB)

Be strong, and let your heart take courage, all you who hope in the Lord. Psalms 31:24 (NASB)

Are not two sparrows sold for a farthing? And one of them shall not fall on the ground without your Father's will. But the very hairs of your head are all numbered. Fear ye not there-

fore, ye are of more value than many sparrows. Matthew 10:30–32 (KJV)

But God was kind! He made me what I am, and his wonderful kindness wasn't wasted. I worked much harder than any of the other apostles, although it was really God's kindness at work and not me. 1 Corinthians 15:10 (CEV)

For God has not given us a spirit of timidity, but of power and love and discipline. 2 Timothy 1:7 (NASB)

For this reason I also suffer these things, but I am not ashamed; for I know whom I have believed and I am convinced that He is able to guard what I have entrusted to Him until that day. 2 Timothy 1:12 (NASB)

So do not throw away your confidence; it will be richly rewarded. Hebrews 10:35 (NIV)

And so we can say with confidence: With the Lord on my side, I fear nothing: what can human beings do to me? Hebrews 13:6 (NJB)

Self-image
(*see also* APPEARANCES *and* CHARACTER)

Wounding strokes are good medicine for evil, blows have an effect on the inmost self. Proverbs 20:30 (NJB)

There is no room for self-delusion. Any one of you who thinks he is wise by worldly standards must learn to be a fool in order to be really wise. 1 Corinthians 3:18 (NJB)

As we have borne the image of the earthly, we shall also bear the image of the heavenly. 1 Corinthians 15:49 (KJV)

We all . . . are changed into the same image from glory to glory, even as by the Spirit of the Lord. 2 Corinthians 3:18 (KJV)

For not he who commends himself is approved, but whom the Lord commends. 2 Corinthians 10:18 (NASB)

I pray that out of his glorious riches he may strengthen you with power through his Spirit in your inner being. Ephesians 3:16 (NIV)

In my inmost self I dearly love God's law. Romans 7:22 (NJB)

And have put on the new self who is being renewed to a true knowledge according to the image of the One who created him—a renewal in which there is no distinction between Greek and Jew, circumcised and uncircumcised, barbarian, Scythian, slave and freeman, but Christ is all, and in all. Colossians 3:10–11 (NASB)

Self-sufficiency
(*see also* DUTY, EMPLOYMENT, RESPONSIBILITY, *and* WORK ETHIC)

You will not be harmed, though thousands fall around you. Psalms 91:7 (CEV)

You will eat the fruit of your labor; blessings and prosperity will be yours. Psalms 128:2 (NIV)

Instruct a wise man and he will be wiser still; teach a righteous man and he will add to his learning. Proverbs 9:9 (NIV)

Train up a child in the way he should go and even when he is old, he will not depart from it. Proverbs 22:6 (KJV)

Those who trust in their own wits are fools, but those who walk in wisdom will come through safely. Proverbs 28:26 (NRSV)

Then this shall be the sign for you: you shall eat this year what grows of itself, in the second year what springs from the same, and in the third year sow, reap, plant vineyards, and eat their fruit. Isaiah 37:30 (NASB)

So if you think you are standing, watch out that you do not fall. 1 Corinthians 10:12 (NRSV)

It is not that we are so competent that we can claim any credit for ourselves; all our competence comes from God. 2 Corinthians 3:5 (NJB)

Remember this: Whoever sows sparingly will also reap sparingly, and whoever sows generously will also reap generously. 2 Corinthians 9:6 (NIV)

I can do everything through him who gives me strength. Philippians 4:13 (NIV)

Silence

Who wants to contest my case? In advance, I agree to be silenced and to die! Job 13:19 (NJB)

A flood of words is never without fault; whoever controls the lips is wise. Proverbs 10:19 (NJB)

Even a fool is thought wise if he keeps silent, and discerning if he holds his tongue. Proverbs 17:28 (NIV)

A time to rend, and a time to sew; a time to keep silence, and a time to speak. Ecclesiastes 3:7 (KJV)

Do not let your mouth lead you into sin. Ecclesiastes 5:6 (NIV)

He was oppressed and He was afflicted, yet He did not open His mouth; like a lamb that is led to slaughter, and like a sheep that is silent before its shearers, so He did not open His mouth. Isaiah 53:7 (NASB)

[Pilate] questioned him in many words; but he answered him nothing. Luke 23:9 (KJV)

Like a lamb before his shearers, so opened he not his mouth. Acts 8:32 (KJV)

For it is God's will that by doing right you should silence the ignorance of the foolish. 1 Peter 2:15 (NRSV)

When the Lamb opened the seventh seal, there was silence in Heaven for about a half an hour. Revelation 8:1 (CEV)

Sin

(*see also* DESIRE, JUDGMENT, MORALITY, RESPONSIBILITY, *and* RESTRAINT)

And when the woman saw that the tree was good for food, and it was pleasant to the eyes, and a tree to be desired to make one wise, she took of the fruit thereof, and did eat, and gave also unto her husband with her; and he did eat. Genesis 3:6 (KJV)

Fathers shall not be put to death for their children, nor children put to death for their fathers; each is to die for his own sin. Deuteronomy 24:16 (NIV)

If iniquity is in your hand, put it far away, and do not let wickedness dwell in your tents. Job 11:14 (NASB)

Remember not the sins of my youth. Psalms 25:7 (KJV)

If thou, Lord, shouldst mark iniquities, O Lord, who

shall stand? Psalms 130:3 (KJV)

Fools mock at the sacrifice for sin, but favor resides among the honest. Proverbs 14:9 (NJB)

Uprightness makes a nation great, by sin whole races are disgraced. Proverbs 14:34 (NJB)

Do not let your mouth lead you into sin. Ecclesiastes 5:6 (NIV)

Surely there is no one on earth so righteous as to do good without ever sinning. Ecclesiastes 7:20 (NRSV)

The Son of man hath power on earth to for-

give sins. Matthew 9:6 (KJV)

And so I tell you, every human sin and blasphemy will be forgiven, but the blasphemy against the Spirit will not be forgiven. Matthew 12:31 (NJB)

Stay awake, and pray not to be put to the test. The spirit is willing enough, but human nature is weak. Matthew 26:41 (NJB)

Forgive us our sins. Luke 11:4 (NRSV)

Everything now covered up will be uncovered, and everything now hidden will be

made clear. Luke 12:2 (NJB)

But when they persisted in asking Him, He straightened up, and said to them, "He who is without sin among you, let him be the first to throw a stone at her." John 8:7 (NASB)

Arise, and be baptized, and wash away thy sins, calling on the name of the Lord. Acts 22:16 (KJV)

Just as by the one man's disobedience the many were made sinners, so by the one man's obedience the many will be made righteous. Romans 5:19 (NRSV)

He who has died is freed from sin. Romans 6:7 (NASB)

For the wages of sin is death, but the free gift of God is eternal life in Christ Jesus our Lord. Romans 6:23 (NRSV)

For I do not do the good I want, but the evil I do not want is what I do. Romans 7:19 (NRSV)

Sin is what gives death its sting, and the Law is the power behind sin. But thank God our Lord Jesus Christ for giving us the victory! 1 Corinthians 15:56–57 (CEV)

You were dead through the trespasses and sins

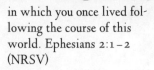

in which you once lived following the course of this world. Ephesians 2:1–2 (NRSV)

Everyone who knows what is the right thing to do and does not do it commits a sin. James 4:17 (NJB)

But if we walk in the light as He himself is in the light, we have fellowship with one another, and the blood of Jesus his son cleanses us from all sin. 1 John 1:7 (NASB)

Whosoever abideth in Him sinneth not: whosoever sinneth hath not seen him, neither known him. 1 John 3:6 (KJV)

Soul

(*see also* DEATH, FAITHFULNESS, LIFE, *and* REDEMPTION)

Man became a living soul. Genesis 2:7 (KJV)

Serve him with all your heart and all your soul. Deuteronomy 11:13 (KJV)

All they that be fat upon earth shall eat and worship: all they that go down to the dust shall bow before him: and none can keep alive his own soul. Psalms 22:29 (KJV)

He restoreth my soul. Psalms 23:3 (KJV)

My soul shall be joyful in the Lord. Psalms 35:9 (KJV)

Bless the Lord, O my soul; and all that is within me bless his holy name. Psalms 103:1 (KJV)

For He has satisfieth the longing soul, and filleth the hungry soul with goodness. Psalms 107:9 (KJV)

Do not fear those who kill the body, but are unable to kill the soul; but rather fear Him who is able to destroy both soul and body in hell. Matthew 10:28 (NASB)

For what is a man profited, if he shall gain the whole world, and lose his own soul? Or what shall a man give in exchange for his soul? Matthew 16:26 (KJV)

For what does it profit a man to gain the whole world, and forfeit his soul? Mark 8:36 (NASB)

It is the spirit that gives life, the flesh has nothing to offer. The words I have spoken to you are spirit and they are life. John 6:63 (NJB)

Anyone who can bring back a sinner from his erring ways will be saving his soul from death and covering over many a sin. James 5:20 (NJB)

You are receiving the outcome of your faith, the salvation of your souls. 1 Peter 1:9 (NRSV)

Strength

The Lord is my strength and my song; he has become my

salvation. He is my God, and I will praise him, my father's God, and I will exalt him. Exodus 15:2 (NIV)

As the man is, so is his strength. Judges 8:21 (KJV)

He keeps the feet of His godly ones, but the wicked ones are silenced in darkness; For not by might shall a man prevail. 1 Samuel 2:9 (NASB)

The joy of the Lord is your strength. Nehemiah 8:10 (KJV)

Has your arm the strength of God's, can your voice thunder as loud? Job 40:9 (NJB)

The Lord is my strength and my shield; my heart trusted in him, and I am helped: therefore my heart greatly rejoiceth; and with my song will I praise him. Psalms 28:7 (NIV)

Cast your burden on the Lord, and he will sustain you. Psalms 55:22 (NRSV)

The wise is mighty in power, strength is reinforced by science. Proverbs 24:5 (NJB)

Wisdom is better than strength. Ecclesiastes 9:16 (NJB)

He gives strength to the weary and increases the power of the weak. Isaiah 40:29 (NIV)

Thou shalt love the Lord thy God . . . with all thy strength. Mark 12:30 (KJV)

God's weakness is stronger than human strength. 1 Corinthians 1:25 (NJB)

And He has said to me, "My grace is sufficient for you, for power is perfected in weakness." Most gladly, therefore, I will rather boast about my weaknesses, that the power of Christ may dwell in me. When I am weak, then am I strong. 2 Corinthians 12:9–10 (KJV)

Stress
(see also ANXIETY, PATIENCE, and TROUBLED TIMES)

I saved your life today, and I pray that the Lord will pro-tect me and keep me safe. 1 Samuel 26:24 (CEV)

The Lord is a refuge for the oppressed, a stronghold in times of trouble. Psalms 9:9 (NIV)

Many are the afflictions of the righteous; but the Lord delivers him out of them all. Psalms 34:19 (NASB)

In my day of distress I call upon you, because you answer me, Lord. Psalms 86:7 (NJB)

We know that all creation is still groaning and is in pain, like a woman about to give birth. The Spirit makes us sure about what we will be in the future. But now we groan silently, while we wait for God to show that

we are his children. This means that our bodies will also be set free. Romans 8:22–23 (CEV)

We often suffer, but we are never crushed. Even when we don't know what to do, we never give up. In times of trouble, God is with us, and when we are knocked down, we get up again. 2 Corinthians 4:8–9 (CEV)

Success

(*see also* AMBITION, FULFILLMENT, GOALS, REWARDS, VICTORY, *and* WEALTH)

This book of the law shall not depart from your mouth, but you shall meditate on it day and night, so that you may be careful to do according to all that is written in it; for then you will make your way prosperous, and then you will have success. Joshua 1:8 (NASB)

Believe in the Lord your God, so shall ye be established; believe his prophets, so shall ye prosper. 2 Chronicles 20:20 (KJV)

If they listen, and serve him, they complete their days in prosperity and their years in pleasantness. Job 36:11 (NRSV)

The upright shall have the land for their own, there they shall live for ever. Psalms 37:29 (NJB)

Hope deferred makes the heart sick, but desire fulfilled is a tree of life. Proverbs 13:12 (NASB)

I then reflected on all that my hands had achieved and all the effort I had put into its achieving. What futility it all was, what chasing after the wind! There is nothing to be gained under the sun. Ecclesiastes 2:11 (NJB)

His power will never end; peace will last forever. He will rule David's kingdom and make it grow strong. He will always rule with honesty and justice. The Lord All-Powerful will make certain that all of this is done. Isaiah 9:7 (CEV)

That's how it is with my words. They don't return to me without doing everything I send them to do. Isaiah 55:11 (CEV)

Everyone will find rest beneath their own fig trees or grape vines, and they will live in peace. This is a solemn promise of the Lord All-Powerful. Micah 4:4 (CEV)

Be on your guard against all kinds of greed; a man's life does not consist in the abundance of his possessions. Luke 12:15 (NIV)

But the Holy Spirit will come upon you and give you power. Then you will tell everyone about me in Jerusalem, in all Judea, in all

Samaria, in all the world. Acts 1:8 (CEV)

In all these things we are more than conquerors through him who loved us. Romans 8:37 (NRSV)

All that matters is that people are telling about Christ, whether they are sincere or not. This is what makes me happy. Philippians 1:18 (CEV)

I did not run in vain or labor in vain. Philippians 2:16 (NRSV)

Suffering
(*see also* GRIEF, TESTS, *and* TROUBLED TIMES)

But he was wounded for our transgressions, he was bruised for our iniquities: the chastisement of our peace was upon him, and with his stripes we are healed. Isaiah 53:5 (KJV)

Though he brings grief, he will show compassion, so great is his unfailing love. Lamentations 3:32 (NIV)

If any want to become my followers, let them deny themselves and take up their cross and follow me. Matthew 16:24 (NRSV)

We must all experience many hardships before we enter the kingdom of God. Acts 14:22 (NJB)

We also rejoice in our sufferings, because we know that suffering produces perseverance; perseverance, character; and character, hope. Romans 5:3–4 (NIV)

For I consider that the sufferings of this present time are not worthy to be compared with the glory that is to be revealed to us. Romans 8:18 (NASB)

And our hope of you is steadfast, knowing, that as ye are partakers of the sufferings, so shall ye be also of the consolation. 2 Corinthians 1:7 (KJV)

For he has graciously granted you privilege not only of believing in Christ, but of suffering for him as well. Philippians 1:29 (NRSV)

He chose to be mistreated with God's people instead of having the good time that sin could bring for a little while. Hebrews 11:25 (CEV)

After all, God chose you to suffer as you follow in the footsteps of Christ, who set an example by suffering for you. 1 Peter 2:21 (CEV)

But even if you do suffer for doing what is right, you are blessed. 1 Peter 3:14 (NRSV)

Christ dies once for our sins. An innocent person dies for those who are guilty. Christ did this to bring you to God, when his body was put to death and his spirit was made alive. 1 Peter 3:18 (CEV)

And the God of all grace, who called you to his eternal glory in Christ, after you have suffered a little while, will himself restore you and make you strong, firm and steadfast. 1 Peter 5:10 (NIV)

Tests

(*see also* PATIENCE, SUFFERING, *and* TROUBLED TIMES)

And Moses said to the people, "Do not be afraid; for God has come in order to test you, and in order that the fear of Him may remain with you, so that you may not sin." Exodus 20:20 (NASB)

What is man, that thou shouldst magnify him? And that thou shouldst set thy heart upon him? And that thou shouldst visit him every morning, and try him every moment?" Job 7:17–18 (KJV)

But He knows the way that I take; when He has tested me, I will come forth as gold. Job 23:10 (NIV)

Prove me, O Lord, and try me; test my heart and mind. Psalms 26:2 (NRSV)

Search me, O God, and know my heart; test me and know my anxious thoughts. Psalms 139:23 (NIV)

Behold, I have refined you, but not as silver; I have tested you in the furnace of affliction. Isaiah 48:10 (NASB)

I, the Lord, search the heart, I test the mind, Even to give to each man according to his ways, According to the results of his deeds. Jeremiah 17:10 (NASB)

Do not put the Lord your God to the test. Matthew 4:7 (NJB)

No temptation has overtaken you but such as is common to man; and God is faithful, who will not allow you to be tempted beyond what you are able, but with the temptation will provide the way of escape also, that you may be able to endure it. 1 Corinthians 10:13 (NASB)

Examine yourselves to see whether you are in the faith; test yourselves. Do you not realize that Christ Jesus is in you—unless, of course, you fail the test? 2 Corinthians 13:5 (NIV)

Prove all things; hold fast to that which is good. 1 Thessalonians 5:21 (KJV)

For the suffering one passed through while being put to

the test enables one to help others when they are being put to the test. Hebrews 2:18 (NJB)

Let no one say when tempted, "I am being tempted by God"; for God cannot be tempted by evil, and does not tempt anyone. James 1:13 (NASB)

Beloved, believe not every spirit, but try the spirits whether they are of God: because many false prophets are gone out into the world. 1 John 4:1 (KJV)

Time

(*see also* THE FUTURE, THE PRESENT, *and* TOMORROW)

For we are but of yesterday and know nothing, because our days upon earth are a shadow. Job 8:9 (KJV)

I will bless the Lord at all times. Psalms 34:1 (KJV)

We can expect seventy years, or maybe eighty, if we are healthy, but even our best years bring trouble and sorrow. Suddenly our time is up, and we disappear. Psalms 90:10 (CEV)

So each of us is to number our days, that we apply our hearts unto wisdom. Psalms 90:12 (KJV)

A generation goes, a generation comes, yet the earth stands firm forever. Ecclesiastes 1:4 (NJB)

The wise, like the fool, will not be long remembered; in days to come both will be forgotten. Like the fool, the wise too must die! Ecclesiastes 2:16 (NIV)

To everything there is a season, and a time to every purpose under heaven. Ecclesiastes 3:1 (KJV)

What is, has been already, what will be, is already; God seeks out anyone who is persecuted. Ecclesiastes 3:15 (NJB)

I again saw under the sun that the race is not to the swift, and the battle is not to the warriors, and neither is bread to the wise, nor wealth to the discerning, nor favor to those of ability; for time and chance overtake them all. Ecclesiastes 9:11 (NASB)

Then I said, "For how long, O Lord?" And he answered: "Until the cities lie ruined and without inhabitant, until the houses are left deserted and the fields ruined and ravaged, until the Lord has sent everyone far away and the land is utterly forsaken. Isaiah 6:11 (CEV)

My hour has not yet come. John 2:4 (CEV)

But when the time was right, God sent his Son, and a woman gave birth to him. Galatians 4:4 (CEV)

But encourage one another daily, as long as it is called Today, so that none of you may be hardened by sin's deceitfulness. Hebrews 3:13 (NIV)

But do not forget this one thing, dear friends: With the Lord a day is like a thousand years, and a thousand years are like a day. 2 Peter 3:8 (NIV)

Tolerance

(see also ACCEPTANCE, JUDGMENT, and MERCY)

Love ye therefore the stranger: for ye were strangers in the land of Egypt. Deuteronomy 10:19 (KJV)

Do not judge lest you be judged. Matthew 7:1 (NASB)

Do not condemn, and you will not be condemned. Luke 6:37 (NJB)

Judge not according to the appearance, but judge righteous judgment. John 7:24 (KJV)

Let not him who eats regard with contempt him who does not eat, and let not him who does not eat judge him who eats, for God has accepted him. Romans 14:3 (NASB)

Accept one another, then, for the sake of God's glory,

as Christ accepted you. Romans 15:7 (NJB)

For ye suffer fools gladly, seeing ye yourselves are wise. 2 Corinthians 11:19 (KJV)

Faith in Jesus Christ is what makes each of you equal with each other, whether you are a Jew or a Greek, a slave or a free person, a man or a woman. Galatians 3:28 (CEV)

Tomorrow

(*see also* THE FUTURE *and* TIME)

Do not congratulate yourself about tomorrow, since you do not know what today will bring forth. Proverbs 27:1 (NJB)

Let us eat and drink, for tomorrow we may die. Isaiah 22:13 (NASB)

"Let me get some wine," . . . drunkards say, "and drink all we can hold! Tomorrow will be even better than today!" Isaiah 56:12 (TEV)

Do not worry about tomorrow: tomorrow will take care of itself. Each day has enough trouble of its own. Matthew 6:34 (NJB)

It is not for you to know the times or the seasons; which the Father hath put in his own power. Acts 1:7 (KJV)

You should know better than to say, "Today or tomorrow we will go to the city. We will do business there for a year and make a lot of money!" What do you know about tomorrow? How can you be so sure about your life? It is nothing but a mist that appears for only a little while before it disappears. James 4:13–15 (CEV)

Tradition

Laban replied, "In our country, the older daughter must get married first. After you spend this week with Leah, you may also marry Rachel. But you will have to work for me another seven years. Genesis 29:26 (CEV)

But Samuel replied: "Does the Lord delight in burnt offerings and sacrifices as much as in obeying the voice of the Lord? To obey is better than sacrifice, and to heed is better than the fat of rams." 1 Samuel 15:22 (NIV)

So while these nations feared the Lord, they also served their idols; their children likewise and their grandchildren, as their fathers

did, so they do to this day. 2 Kings 17:41 (NASB)

This is what the Lord says: "Stand at the crossroads and look; ask for the ancient paths, ask where the good way is, and walk in it, and you will find rest for your souls." But you said, "We will not walk in it." Jeremiah 6:16 (NIV)

You have heard that it was said to those of ancient times "Do not murder" and "A murderer must be brought to trial." But I say to you that if you are angry with someone, you will have to stand trial. If you call someone a fool, you will be taken to court. And if you say that someone is worthless, you will be in danger of the fires of hell. Matthew 5:21–22 (NRSV)

"Why do your disciples break the tradition of the elders? They don't wash their hands before they eat!" Jesus replied, "Why do you break the command of God for the sake of your tradition?" Matthew 15:2–3 (NRSV)

So, for the sake of your tradition, you make void the word of God. Matthew 5:16 (NRSV)

You put aside the commandment of God to observe human traditions. Mark 7:8 (NJB)

Ye stiff-necked and uncircumcised in heart and ears; ye do always resist the Holy Ghost: as your fathers did, so do ye. Acts 7:51 (KJV)

Troubled Times

(*see also* DISAPPOINTMENT, FAITHFULNESS, GRIEF, HOPE, PRAYER, SUFFERING, *and* TESTS)

Be strong . . . fear not, nor be afraid of them: for the Lord thy God, that doth go with thee; will not fail thee, nor forsake thee. Deuteronomy 31:6 (KJV)

Do not tremble or be dismayed, for the Lord your God is with you wherever you go. Joshua 1:9 (NRSV)

As surely as I valued your life today, so may the Lord value my life and deliver me from all trouble. 1 Samuel 26:24 (NIV)

God is our refuge and strength, a very present help in trouble. Psalms 46:1 (NRSV)

In the day of distress I call upon you, because you answer me, Lord. Psalms 86:7 (NJB)

Hide not thy face from me in the day when I am in trouble; incline thine ear

unto me: in the day when I call answer me speedily. Psalms 102:2 (KJV)

The Lord preserves the simple; I was brought low, and He saved me. Psalms 116:6 (NASB)

Though I walk in the midst of trouble, Thou wilt revive me; Thou wilt stretch forth Thy hand against the wrath of my enemies, and Thy right hand will save me. Psalms 138:7 (NASB)

If you falter in times of trouble, how small is your strength! Proverbs 24:10 (NIV)

God hath put us to silence, and given us water of gall to drink, because we have sinned against the Lord. We looked for peace, but no good came, and for a time of health, and behold trouble! Jeremiah 8:14b–15 (KJV)

The Lord is good, a stronghold in the day of trouble, and He knows those who take refuge in Him. Nahum 1:7 (NASB)

None of the trials which have come upon you is more than a human being can stand. You can trust that God will not let you be put to the test beyond your strength, but with any trial will also provide a way out by enabling you to put up with it. 1 Corinthians 10:13 (NJB)

Blessed be God, even the Father of our Lord Jesus Christ, the Father of mercies, and God of all comfort;

who comforteth us in all our tribulation, that we may be able to comfort them which are in any trouble, by the comfort wherewith we ourselves are comforted of God. 2 Corinthians 1:3–4 (KJV)

Trust

(*see also* COMMITMENT, FAITHFULNESS, PROTECTION, *and* SUFFERING)

But if He thus say, I have no delight in thee; behold, here am I, let Him to do to me as seemeth good unto Him. 2 Samuel 15:26 (KJV)

Some call on chariots, some on horses, but we on the name of the Lord our God. Psalms 20:7 (NJB)

Blessed is the man who makes the Lord his trust, who does not look to the proud, to those who turn aside to false gods. Psalms 40:4 (NIV)

In God I will praise his word, in God I have put my trust; I will not fear what flesh can do unto me. Psalms 56:4 (KJV)

Trust in Him at all times. Psalms 62:8 (KJV)

Surely God is my salvation; I will trust, and will not be afraid, for the Lord God is my strength and my might; he has become my salvation. Isaiah 12:2 (NRSV)

When you cry out for help, let your collection of idols save you! The wind will carry all of them off, a mere breath will blow them away. But the man who makes me his refuge will inherit the land and possess my holy mountain. Isaiah 57:13 (NIV)

Thus saith the Lord; Cursed be the man that trusteth in man, and maketh flesh his arm, and whose heart departeth from the Lord. Jeremiah 17:5 (KJV)

Truth
(*see also* HONESTY)

As the Lord liveth, what the Lord saith unto me, that will I speak. 1 Kings 22:14 (KJV)

Those who walk blamelessly, and do what is right, speak the truth from their hearts. Psalms 15:2 (NRSV)

Send out your light and your truth; let them lead me. Psalms 43:3 (NRSV)

The Lord is near to all who call on him, to all who call on him in truth. Psalms 145:18 (NRSV)

For His loving kindness is great toward us, And the truth of the Lord is everlasting. Praise the Lord! Psalms 117:2 (NASB)

Buy the truth, and sell it not. Proverbs 23:23 (KJV)

But you must be truthful with each other, and in court you must give fair decisions that lead to peace. Zechariah 8:16 (CEV)

Sky and earth will pass away, but my words will not pass away. Mark 13:31 (NJB)

But he who practices the truth comes to the light, that his deeds may be manifested as having been wrought in God. John 3:21 (NASB)

And ye shall know the truth, and the truth shall make you free. John 8:32 (KJV)

Jesus answered, "I am the way and the truth and the life. No one comes to the Father except through me." John 14:6 (NIV)

When he, the Spirit of truth, is come, he will guide you into all truth. John 16:13 (KJV)

"So you are a king," Pilate replied. "You are saying that I am a king," Jesus told him. "I was born into this world to tell about the truth. And everyone who belongs to the truth knows my voice." Pilate asked Jesus, "What is truth?" John 18:37–38 (CEV)

Am I therefore become your enemy, because I tell you the truth? Galatians 4:16 (KJV)

Surely you heard . . . and were taught . . . in accordance with the truth that is in Jesus. Ephesians 4:21 (NIV)

Finally . . . let your minds be filled with everything that is true, everything that is honorable, everything that is upright and pure, everything that we love and admire—with whatever is good and praiseworthy. Philippians 4:8 (NJB)

He that saith, I know Him and keepeth not his commandments, is a liar, and the truth is not in him. 1 John 2:4 (KJV)

I have no greater joy than to hear that my children walk in the truth. 3 John 4 (KJV)

I saw heaven standing open and there before me was a white horse, whose rider is called Faithful and True. With justice he judges and makes war. Revelation 19:11 (NIV)

The Unknowable
(*see also* DESTINY *and* FAITHFULNESS)

The secret things belong unto the Lord our God: but those things which are revealed belong unto us and to our children for ever, that we may do all the words of this law. Deuteronomy 29:29 (KJV)

Can you find out the deep things of God? Can you find out the limit of the Almighty? Job 11:7 (NRSV)

How great God is—God is more than we imagine; no one can count the years he has lived. Job 36:26 (CEV)

Such amazing knowledge is beyond me, a height to which I cannot attain. Psalms 139:6 (NJB)

But there is a God in heaven that revealeth secrets, and maketh known . . . what shall be in the latter days. Daniel 2:28 (KJV)

The wind bloweth where it listeth, and thou hearest the sound thereof, but canst not tell whence it cometh, and whither it goeth: so is every one that is born of the Spirit. John 3:8 (KJV)

It is not for you to know times or dates that the Father has decided by His own authority. Acts 1:7 (NJB)

Oh, the depth of the riches both of the wisdom and knowledge of God! How unsearchable are His judgments and unfathomable His ways! Romans 11:33 (NASB)

What no one ever saw or heard, what no one ever thought could happen, is the very thing God prepared for those who love him. 1 Corinthians 2:9 (TEV)

For who has known the mind of the Lord so as to instruct Him? 1 Corinthians 2:16 (NRSV)

For we know in part, and we prophesy in part. 1 Corinthians 13:9 (KJV)

For now we see through a glass, darkly; but then face to face: now I know in part; but then shall I know even as I am known. 1 Corinthians 13:12 (KJV)

God is greater than our hearts, and he knows everything. 1 John 3:20 (NIV)

And I saw a strong angel proclaiming with a loud voice, "Who is worthy to open the book and to break its seals?" Revelation 5:2 (NASB)

Values

(*see also* GOALS, MONEY, PRIORITIES, *and* WEALTH)

Give not that which is holy unto the dogs, neither cast ye your pearls before swine, lest they trample them under their feet, and turn and rend against you. Matthew 7:6 (KJV)

He said to them, "You are the ones who pass yourselves off as upright in people's sight, but God knows your hearts. For what is highly esteemed in human eyes is loathsome in the sight of God." Luke 16:15 (NJB)

Do not work for food that spoils, but for food that endures to eternal life, which the Son of Man will give you. On him God the Father has placed His seal of approval. John 6:27 (NIV)

While we look not at the things which are seen, but at the things which are not seen; for the things which are seen are temporal, but the things which are not seen are eternal. 2 Corinthians 4:18 (NASB)

Over all these clothes, put on love, the perfect bond. Colossians 3:14 (NJB)

Prove all things; hold fast that which is good. 1 Thessalonians 5:21 (KJV)

Adulterers! Do you not realize that love for the world is hatred for God? Anyone who chooses the world for a friend is constituted an enemy of God. James 4:4 (NJB)

Victory

(*see also* FULFILLMENT *and* SUCCESS)

Then Moses and the sons of Israel sang this song to the Lord, and said, I will sing to the Lord, for He is highly exalted; The horse and its rider He has hurled into the sea. Exodus 15:1 (NASB)

And it came about at the seventh time, when the priests blew the trumpets, Joshua said to the people, "Shout! For the Lord has given you the city." Joshua 6:16 (NASB)

The triumphing of the wicked is short. Job 20:5 (KJV)

Sing to the Lord a new song, for he has done marvelous

things; his right hand and his holy arm have worked salvation for him. Psalms 98:1 (NIV)

The Lord said unto my Lord, "Sit thou at my right hand, until I make thine enemies thy footstool." Psalms 110:1 (KJV)

This is the day the Lord has made; let us rejoice and be glad in it. Psalms 118:24 (NIV)

The horse is prepared for the day of battle, but victory belongs to the Lord. Proverbs 21:31 (NASB)

He will swallow up death in victory. Isaiah 25:8 (KJV)

I have told you all this so that you may find peace in me. In the world you will have hardship, but be courageous: I have conquered the world. John 16:33 (NJB)

We come through all these things triumphantly victorious, by the power of him who loved us. Romans 8:37 (NJB)

So when this incorruptible shall have out on in corruption, and this mortal shall have put on immortality, then shall be brought to pass the saying that is written, Death is swallowed up in victory. O death, where is thy sting? O grave, where is thy victory? 1 Corinthians 15:54-55 (KJV)

But thanks be to God! He gives us the victory through

our Lord Jesus Christ.
1 Corinthians 15:57
(NIV)

For everyone born of
God overcomes the
world. This is the vic-
tory that has overcome
the world, even our
faith. 1 John 5:4 (NIV)

Be faithful until death
and I will give you the
crown of life. Revela-
tion 2:10 (NRSV)

Anyone who proves
victorious will inherit
these things; and I will
be his God and he will
be my son. Revelation
21:7 (NJB)

Virtue

(*see also* GOODNESS,
HONESTY, *and* RIGHT-
EOUSNESS)

Believe me, God nei-
ther spurns anyone of
integrity, nor lends his
aid to the evil. Job
8:20 (NJB)

God, create in me a clean
heart, renew within me
a resolute spirit. Psalms
51:10 (NJB)

Once again Jesus spoke
to the people. This
time he said, "I am the
light for the world!
Follow me, and you
won't be walking in
the dark. You will have
the light that gives
life." John 8:12 (CEV)

Finally, brothers, let your minds be filled with everything that is true, everything that is honorable, everything that is upright and pure, everything that we love and admire—with whatever is good and praiseworthy. Philippians 4:8 (NJB)

But let us, who are of the day, be sober, putting on the breastplate of faith and love; and for an helmet, the hope of salvation. 1 Thessalonians 5:8 (KJV)

According as his divine power hath given unto us all things that pertain unto life and godliness, through the knowledge of him that hath called us to glory and virtue: Whereby are given to us exceeding great and precious promises . . . besides this, giving all diligence, add to your faith virtue, and to your virtue knowledge. 2 Peter 1:3, 5 (KJV)

Visions
(*see also* DREAMS)

I saw in the night visions, and behold, one like the Son of Man came with the clouds of heaven. Daniel 7:13 (KJV)

. . . I had a vision of the Lord. He was on his throne high above, and his robe filled the temple. Flaming creatures with six wings were flying over him. They covered their faces with two of their wings and their bodies with two more. They used the other two wings for flying, as they shouted, "Holy, holy, holy, Lord All-Powerful! The earth is filled with your glory." Isaiah 6:1–3 (CEV)

Six days later Jesus took Peter and the brothers James and John with him. They went up on a very high mountain where they could be alone. There in front of the disciples, Jesus was completely changed. His face was shining like the sun, and his face became white as light . . . the shadow of a bright cloud passed over them. From the cloud a voice said, "This is my own dear Son, and I am pleased with him. Listen to what he says!" Matthew 17:1–2, 5 (CEV)

In the last days, God says, I will pour out my Spirit on all people. Your sons and daughters will prophesy, your young men will see visions, your old men will dream dreams. Acts 2:17 (NIV)

Behold, I see the heavens opened up and the Son of Man standing at the right hand of God. Acts 7:56 (NASB)

And a vision appeared to Paul in the night . . . And after he had seen the vision, immediately we endeavored to go to Macedonia, assuredly gathering that the Lord had called us for to preach the gospel unto them. Acts 16:9–10 (KJV)

For now we see in a glass, darkly; but then face to face: now I know in part; but then shall I know even as also I am known. 1 Corinthians 13:12 (KJV)

Wealth

(*see also* MONEY *and* VALUES)

You may say to yourself, "My power and the strength of my hands have produced this wealth for me." But remember the Lord your God, for it is He who gives you the ability to produce wealth, and so confirms His covenant, which He swore to your forefathers, as it is today. Deuteronomy 8:17–18 (NIV)

Moreover, I will give you what you have not asked for—both riches and honor—so that in your lifetime you will have no equal among kings. 1 Kings 3:13 (NIV)

Wealth and honor come from you; you are the ruler of all things. In your hands are strength and power to exalt

and give strength to all.
1 Chronicles 29:12 (NIV)

Likewise all to whom God
gives wealth and possessions
and whom he enables to enjoy
them, and to accept their lot
and find enjoyment in their
toil—this is the gift of God.
Ecclesiastes 5:19 (NRSV)

A little that a righteous man
hath is better than the riches
of many wicked. Psalms
37:16 (KJV)

Trust not in oppression, and
become not vain in robbery:
if riches increase, set not
your heart upon them.
Psalms 62:10 (KJV)

For I envied the arrogant
when I saw the prosperity of
the wicked. Psalms 73:3
(NIV)

In the day of retribution,
riches will be useless, but
uprightness delivers from
death. Proverbs 11:4 (NJB)

Whoever trusts in riches
will have a fall, the upright
will flourish like the leaves.
Proverbs 11:28 (NJB)

Wealth hastily gotten will
dwindle, but those who
gather little by little will
increase it. Proverbs 13:11
(NRSV)

In the house of the upright
there is no lack of treasure;
the earnings of the wicked
are fraught with anxiety.
Proverbs 15:6 (NJB)

Better have little and with it
uprightness than great rev-
enues with injustice.
Proverbs 16:8 (NJB)

For where your treasure is, there your heart will be also. Matthew 6:21 (NIV)

And Jesus said to His disciples, "Truly I say to you, it is hard for a rich man to enter the kingdom of heaven. It is easier for a camel to go through the eye of a needle than a rich man to enter the kingdom of God." Matthew 19:23–24 (NRSV)

But woe to you who are rich, for you are receiving your comfort in full. Luke 6:24 (NASB)

For we brought nothing into the world, and it is certain we can carry nothing out. 1 Timothy 6:7 (KJV)

But those who want to be rich fall into temptation and are trapped by many senseless and harmful desires that plunge people into ruin and destruction. For the love of money is the root of all kinds of evil. 1 Timothy 6:9–10 (NRSV)

Wisdom

(*see also* LEARNING *and* LISTENING)

He said [to the judges]: "Be careful when you make your decisions in court, because these are the Lord's people, and he will know what you decide." 2 Chronicles 19:6 (CEV)

Coral and jasper are not worthy of mention; the price

of wisdom is beyond rubies. Job 28:18 (NIV)

And unto man he said, "Behold, the fear of the Lord, that is wisdom; and to depart from evil is understanding." Job 28:28 (KJV)

Age should speak; advanced years should teach wisdom. Job 32:7 (NIV)

Respect and obey the Lord! This is the beginning of knowledge. Only a fool rejects wisdom and good advice. Proverbs 1:7 (CEV)

Do not be wise in your own eyes; fear the Lord and turn away from evil. Proverbs 3:7 (NASB)

Wisdom is the principal thing; therefore get wisdom: and with all thy getting get understanding. Proverbs 4:7 (KJV)

How much better to get wisdom than gold, to choose understanding rather than silver! Proverbs 16:16 (NIV)

Better a poor but wise youth than an old but foolish king who no longer knows how to take warning. Ecclesiastes 4:13 (NIV)

Wisdom is a shelter as money is a shelter, but the advantage of knowledge is this: that wisdom preserves the life of its possessor. Ecclesiastes 7:12 (NIV)

Wisdom is better than strength. Ecclesiastes 9:16 (KJV)

There is no room for self-delusion. Any one of you who thinks he is wise by worldly standards must learn to be a fool in order to be really wise. For the wisdom of this world is foolishness with God. 1 Corinthians 3:18 (NJB)

If any of you needs wisdom, you should ask God, and it will be given to you. God is generous and won't correct you for asking. James 1:5 (CEV)

Work Ethic

(*see also* EMPLOYMENT, PERSEVERANCE, RESPONSIBILITY, *and* SELF-SUFFICIENCY)

Do your work in six days and rest on the seventh day, even during the seasons for plowing and harvesting. Exodus 34:21 (CEV)

There, in the presence of the Lord your God, you and your families shall eat and shall rejoice in everything you have put your hand to, because the Lord your God has blessed you. Deuteronomy 12:7 (NIV)

I pray that the Lord God of Israel will reward you for what you have done. And now that you have come to him for protection, I pray that he will bless you. Ruth 2:12 (CEV)

But you, be strong and do not lose courage, for there is

reward for your work.
2 Chronicles 15:7
(NASB)

Then I told them how
kind God had been and
what the king had said.
Immediately they
replied, "Let's start
building now!" So they
got everything ready.
Nehemiah 2:18 (CEV)

Anyone unwilling to
work should not eat.
Psalms 90:17 (NRSV)

You shall eat the fruit
of the labor of your
hands. Psalms 128:2
(NRSV)

Lazy hands make a man
poor, but diligent
hands bring wealth.
Proverbs 10:4 (NIV)

You see someone alert
at his business? His aim
will be to serve kings;
not for him the service
of the obscure.
Proverbs 22:29 (NJB)

And all that my eyes
desired I did not refuse
them. I did not with-
hold my heart from any
pleasure, for my heart
was pleased because of
all my labor and this
was my reward for all
my labor. Ecclesiastes
2:10 (NASB)

I see there is no con-
tentment for a human
being except happiness
in achievement; such is
the lot of all human
beings. No one can tell
us what will happen

after we are gone.
Ecclesiastes 3:22 (NJB)

If you have to work hard for a living, you can rest well at night even if you don't have much to eat. But if you are rich, you can't even sleep. Ecclesiastes 5:12 (CEV)

Whatever your hand finds to do, do it with all your might, for in the grave, where you are going, there is neither working nor planning nor knowledge nor wisdom. Ecclesiastes 9:10 (NIV)

Now he that planteth and he that watereth are one: and every man shall receive his own reward according to his own labor. 1 Corinthians 3:8 (KJV)

For we hear that some of you are living in idleness, mere busybodies, not doing any work. Now such persons we command and exhort in Jesus Christ to do their work quietly and to earn their own living. 2 Thessalonians 3:11–12 (NRSV)

It is just as the Scriptures say, "Don't muzzle an ox when you are using it to grind grain." You also know the saying, "Workers are worth their pay." 1 Timothy 5:18 (CEV)

Worship

(*see also* PRAISING GOD *and* PRAYER)

Then Moses and the Israelites sang this song to the Lord: I will sing to the Lord, for he is highly exalted. The horse and its rider he has hurled into the sea. Exodus 15:1 (NIV)

And thou shalt love the Lord thy God with all thine heart, and with all thy soul, and with all thy might. Deuteronomy 6:5 (KJV)

But the Lord, who brought you up from the land of Egypt with great power and with an outstretched arm, Him you shall fear, and to Him you shall bow yourselves down, and to Him you shall sacrifice. 2 Kings 17:36 (NASB)

I will wash mine hands in innocency: so will I compass thine altar, O Lord: that I may publish with the voice of thanksgiving, and tell of all thy wondrous works. Psalms 26:6–7 (KJV)

Bow down and worship the Lord our Creator! The Lord is our God, and we are his people, the sheep he takes care of in his own pasture. Psalms 95:6–7 (CEV)

Everyone on earth, now tremble and worship the Lord, majestic and holy. Psalms 96:9 (CEV)

Praise the Lord! Praise the Lord from the heavens;

Praise Him in the heights!
Psalms 148:1 (NASB)

Let everything that has
breath praise the Lord.
Praise the Lord! Alleluia!
Psalms 150:6 (NASB)

For faithful love is what
pleases me, not sacrifice;
knowledge of God, not burnt
offerings. Hosea 6:6 (NJB)

Worship the Lord your God
and serve only Him! Luke
4:8 (CEV)

Therefore, since we receive a
kingdom which cannot be
shaken, let us show gratitude, by which we may offer
to God an acceptable service
with reverence and awe!
Hebrews 12:28 (NASB)

Who will not fear thee, O
Lord, and glorify thy name?
For thou only art holy: for
all nations shall come and
worship before thee; for thy
judgments are made mani-
fest. Revelation 15:4 (KJV)